PICKETS AND DEAD MEN

PICKETS AND DEAD MEN

Seasons on Rainier

BREE LOEWEN

THE MOUNTAINEERS BOOKS

THE MOUNTAINEERS BOOKS
*is the nonprofit publishing arm of The Mountaineers Club, an
organization founded in 1906 and dedicated to the exploration,
preservation, and enjoyment of outdoor and wilderness areas.*

1001 SW Klickitat Way, Suite 201, Seattle, WA 98134

First edition, 2009

Manufactured in the United States of America

Developmental Editor: Julie Van Pelt
Copy Editor: Carol Poole
Cover Design: Karen Schober
Book Design and Layout: Mayumi Thompson

Cover artwork: Jannelle Loewen

Library of Congress Cataloging-in-Publication Data
Loewen, Bree, 1981-
  Pickets and dead men / by Bree Loewen. — 1st ed.
    p. cm.
  ISBN-13: 978-1-59485-101-8
  ISBN-10: 1-59485-101-8
  1. Mountaineering—Search and rescue operations—Washington (State)—
Rainier, Mount. 2. Park rangers—Washington (State)—Mount Rainier National
Park. 3. Loewen, Bree, 1981- I. Title.
  GV200.183.L63 2009
  363.14'09797782—dc22
                          2008028361

CONTENTS

ACKNOWLEDGMENTS

GEORGE BURNS ONCE SAID, "No snowflake in an avalanche ever feels responsible." Here's a shout out to all the unique and multi-faceted individuals who are responsible for the creation of this book. Thanks to Ted, Adrienne, Tracie, Tom, Paul, Charlie, and the rest of the park folk for giving me the awesome experience of having met and worked with you. You guys have changed my life in so many ways. Thanks to my friends and climbing partners Alice, Ryan, and Russell, who taught me how important grace is in climbing and in life. Thanks to the entire staff of the Mountaineers Books for their time and attention. It was a pleasure to work with Dana Youlin, Mary Metz, Julie Van Pelt, and Carol Poole. Special thanks to Russell for your unfailing support on this project, as well as for marrying me and giving me a child and a small house in the country with nice Adirondack chairs, a big kitchen, and a spot to grow organic peas. Happy endings are the best.

AUTHOR'S NOTE

I HAVE MADE EVERY EFFORT TO PROVIDE an accurate account of the people, places, and events as relating to my experiences on Rainier. I have relied on my own memory and journals, as well as the memories of friends, family, and fellow rangers. But essentially this is my story, my perspective on my seasons on Rainier. Any gaps in my story or misrepresentation of facts are purely accidental and unintentional. In most cases, I have confirmed or attempted to confirm such details, but there will undoubtedly be a few inconsistencies, for which I apologize in advance. Some individuals' names have been changed.

1

DON'T GET FROSTBITE

A MONTH INTO MY FIRST SEASON I was interviewed by the *Tacoma News Tribune* about what it was like to be a girl climbing ranger at Mount Rainier National Park. They wanted to know about my typical day, how many people I'd rescued, and what it felt like to kick butt in the mountains wearing a sports bra and floral print shorts. I told them the bra and shorts were buried under too many layers of clothing to be a factor. I said sometimes it was difficult being a woman in the profession, but other things were far more difficult, and then, laughing, I told the reporter I wasn't going to talk about any of it because being a climbing ranger was my dream job and I wanted to keep it.

As I understand it, when I was hired there were several guys who had been volunteering as climbing rangers for years with the expectation that they would get hired as soon as spots opened up. They'd had a falling out with the boss just before the season started, despite being well-liked and respected by everyone else. Consequently, they were slighted when myself and two other girls with no real experience on the mountain whatsoever were hired in their places.

We three girls had a poor understanding of what we were supposed to be doing on a daily basis. Almost no one wanted to invest the time to teach us how to do our jobs right, and no one expected us to stay very long. In the beginning, I persisted partly because of the glamorous idea of doing high-profile rescues. I wanted to fly around in helicopters and watch my work on the evening news. Mostly, though, I thought shared hardship increased camaraderie, and so the more difficult and stressful rescues I took part in, the less the grudges of the past would matter, and the closer a community my coworkers and I would become. I wanted to create friendships that would last, that I could trust my life to, the kind where we would sit together when we were old and reminisce about all the crazy things we'd done.

These friendships never really materialized, but I stayed for years anyway because of my relationship with the public and the beauty of the environment, and because I received a paycheck. Among my coworkers, I was the one who cleaned the bathroom, but when I was the lone ranger on the upper mountain I was the ultimate voice of authority. When people did what I said, they lived, and when they didn't, they died, or at least suffered unreasonably. They didn't always respect my advice at the time, or sometimes ever come to appreciate the unconditional support I gave them, but I knew even the small contributions I was able to provide were making an immediate difference in the lives of inexperienced or unlucky climbers every day. Although these weren't the types of relationships I was looking for when I started, I recognized that they were important nonetheless.

This do-gooder desire was combined with my lack of other job prospects. I'd graduated from college at seventeen with a philosophy degree, spent the next four years as a climbing bum living in my compact car, and had most recently worked as an ambulance jockey, sleeping on the gurney in the back between unlimited overtime shifts. That was a job that I would have done almost anything not to go back to because I felt like the longer I worked there, the more jaded I became towards the people I was sent to help. I saw starving old people who were afraid to tell anybody, and babies covered in rat bites, along with a litany of things that seemed to me to be worse than death. I saw so much that things that should have bothered me started not to. I didn't want to be numb. I wanted to be compassionate and understanding again, and I wanted my days to be filled with beauty and success.

This left me at age twenty-one with climbing as my only job skill, and I'd just had one of the rare, extremely hard-to-get climbing-based jobs dropped in my lap. Here I was, with important work handed to me every day in one of the most beautiful places on earth. I wanted to prove I had what it took to work every day in the mountains, to show that women could excel at this work. I didn't want to blow it.

During my three seasons at Rainier I came to realize that, as much as I wanted to prove myself, in the end I didn't have the skills or stamina to live up to the standards my supervisors, coworkers, and the public set for me, let alone the ones I set for myself.

Even from day one, things were grim. I came into the job with a debilitating reputation to overcome: I'd been rescued off Mount Rainier in a highly televised extravaganza less than a month before I got hired to rescue others.

This is how it happened. I was planning to climb Denali with two friends, Alice and Cicily. A few years earlier, Cicily and I had met while working in an outdoor goods shop, paying our way through college, but we'd never climbed a mountain together. So, only a week after I submitted my application to be a climbing ranger, Cicily and I decided we should climb something smaller and local first to make sure we could get along on a big trip. Since the majority of our climbing experience had been on alpine rock, Mount Rainier seemed like the perfect choice for honing our slogging skills.

February was when Cicily could get away, so on Valentine's Day I picked her up and we drove to Mount Rainier, our practice climb, in a torrential rainstorm. By the time we reached Paradise at the end of the road on the mountain's south side, the rain had turned to snow and sleet, and the wind had picked up. It was horrible weather for climbing, and we sat in the car with the heater running, watching the slush land on the windshield, trying to work up the guts to get out of the car.

We'd planned on doing Gibraltar Ledges, a standard winter route, but the weather shrank our aspirations to just hiking to the public shelter, a heatless rock building at Camp Muir about halfway up the mountain. We figured we'd hang out for a few days, which in my mind meant we'd be cold and wet and miserable together—a good test of whether we'd be able to do it again for a longer period of time.

I was really excited to finally be putting together an international women's trip. My previous trip—leading climbs in Peru without pay for an under-the-table guiding business run by my ex-boyfriend, who'd tried to strangle me with a tent cord one night when I ate more than my meager share of freeze-dried pineapple chicken and rice—had been lousy. The climbing had been fantastic, but the social dynamic had been too scary to make it worthwhile. I wanted to have a climbing experience that involved both amazing climbing and fun partners, and this Rainier trip seemed like a good idea to make sure all would go OK on Denali. I really wanted the Alaska climb to be a bonding experience. I wanted to forge a long-lasting climbing partnership with Cicily, to grow up and grow old with her and Alice. I wanted us to be able to trust each other with everything, and do epic, amazing routes together in the future. I just knew that Rainier and then Denali would be the catalysts that would make it all happen. In retrospect, my expectations might have been too high.

We got our backcountry permit and started hiking up through the snow play area, which was almost deserted in the hideous weather. Cicily started having problems right away. She said her backpack was rubbing on her shoulders, and her mouth turned down like she was about to cry. I was glad for the sideways sleet, because it prevented me from seeing if she was tearing up. I was afraid that a breakdown this early, before we were comfortable with each other, might lead more to awkwardness than camaraderie. I asked if there was anything I could do, since I'd done a lot of pack fittings at the outdoor shop and I knew people often underutilized their load straps. She asked me if I could take some of the weight. I was surprised, but I knew I could carry it so I didn't mind too much.

We stopped and took off our backpacks, and then she handed me the stove and pot, the rest of the group gear, and two quart-size bottles of contact-lens solution. I didn't say anything, but secretly worried that since I hadn't even brought a toothbrush I had misjudged the hygiene standards of this trip. I packed for light and fast style, which usually meant I reeked after a few days. My usual climbing partner, Alice, had never cared, but I wondered now if she had just put up with me all these years, if I was unaware of some female backcountry grooming code.

Cicily and I shouldered our packs again, but in another hundred yards she stopped and said it was the pack itself that was the problem. I grinned, "Do you want to switch packs?" Five minutes later I had all the gear inside her pack. I hoisted it up and we were off again. I was having a really good time despite the weather, and the pack thing didn't seem like a big deal. I knew that girl climbing partners are hard to find. I was willing to carry the contact lens solution. I was willing to be flexible and forgiving no matter what happened because I wanted this trip to work, and I hoped Cicily would, too.

After we passed tree line, the already poor visibility deteriorated rapidly. At first I could see about a hundred yards, but that dropped to a few feet in the encroaching whiteout. I was squinting, unable to keep more than one eye open against the wet ice crystals the wind was blasting in my face. My hood was cinched as tight as it would go, but water was still running down the back of my neck from the snow blowing in. I realized I was going to be cold and wet all the way to Camp Muir, but I wasn't too worried about finding the way there. I had a map and compass, and I was fairly sure we'd find the shelter as long as we followed the bearings.

We had seen a few other hardy souls around Paradise, but as we got higher only two men looked like they were continuing up the mountain. Cicily was lagging a ways behind me, so I would plod along for a while, then stop and wait so we didn't lose each other. One of the two men was also stopping to wait for his companion, and the two of us were leapfrogging. I felt anti-social staying so close to them but not saying anything, so the next time he passed me I yelled, "Hi!" and waved.

He came over and said his name was Steve. He looked to be in his late fifties and fairly weathered, though his hood hid most of his face. He seemed nice enough, and extremely confident in his climbing abilities. Shouting to be heard over the wind, he named a number of Alaskan summits he'd been to, which made sense because he said he lived in Anchorage. He'd come to summit Rainier via Gibraltar Ledges with his long-lost college friend, Kim. They had wanted to climb together, but the trip's real purpose was to be one of Kim's training climbs for Mount Everest.

I was happy to talk to Steve, but I was wearing every bit of clothing I had and I was freezing. I was beginning to get impatient and tired of doing jumping jacks on the long stops. I remember wishing Cicily would hurry so we could get to the shelter before dark, but a few hours later, in the dark, with the wind blowing so hard it was nearly knocking Cicily and me off our snowshoes (the guys didn't have snowshoes), we couldn't find the shelter. Steve had an altimeter and he kept yelling that we were at the right elevation, but that the shelter was missing. I doubted this, but since I couldn't find it, either, it seemed easier to accept that the shelter was missing than that we were lost. We decided to dig in where we were and spend the night, since the weather was too awful either to keep looking for the shelter or to turn back.

Steve and Kim's plan had been to do Gibraltar Ledges in a single push—a burly goal in winter—and they hadn't brought a lot of gear. Cicily and I had planned on spending the night in the shelter. So none of us had a tent. We talked about digging a snow cave, but because January that year had been sunny, there was a bulletproof ice layer about two feet down, covered by loose, un-consolidated snow. I had the only shovel and it was no match for the ice layer, so I dug a trench a few feet deep and wide enough for the four of us and we just lay down next to each other. Cicily and Kim had bivy sacks. I was still saving money to buy one. My down sleeping bag filled with snow the instant I unzipped it to get in, and knowing that the bag would be worthless once the snow melted into the down, I got into it with my full raingear and boots still on. I didn't really mind the unplanned night out in a big storm. I was happy whether we got ourselves in trouble or not, since the point of the trip was to find out how Cicily and I got along in tense situations. I was just excited to see how we did before it really counted.

It was a sleepless night. The storm was warm and wet, and several feet of heavy new snow fell. The winds increased. At first light, we got up because we were freezing and our sleeping bags were useless. None of us had put our water bottles in our sleeping bags, which was stupid, because now they were chock-full of ice. None of us ate anything or even commented about the lack of water because we wanted to begin moving down immediately, thinking we were only a few hours away from the parking lot.

I got out the map and compass. We didn't know exactly where we were, but we thought we were close to Camp Muir. I wanted to follow the cheat-sheet bearings the ranger station had handed out, but after walking a few hundred yards—Cicily and I breaking trail with our snowshoes, the two men behind, postholing in our footsteps—Cicily started freaking out, saying we were going to die in an avalanche. Some rime ice-covered rocks on our left looked like they paralleled us on a bit of a ridge, and she wanted to follow the rocks down instead, thinking it was a safer route.

It turned into a bit of an argument between us. I was fine with an unplanned night out, but I was ready to go back to the car. I said if we followed the rocks down, we'd be completely lost, since we didn't know what rocks they were, but if we stayed on the bearings we'd be OK. I didn't think the snowfield was steep enough to slide. Cicily said she knew we'd be caught in an avalanche if we stayed on the bearings, and said she'd follow the rocks down by herself if she had to.

I remember yelling, "Cicily, if we go that way we're going to be in for a major epic!" But I also felt that we couldn't split up. I didn't want to lose a friend and potentially good climbing partner because of a stupid fight. I also had all of Cicily's clothes and equipment in my pack. I resolved that a major epic would be OK—at least I'd get to know her. Maybe we could still have a quality bonding experience.

The two men behind us didn't say anything about what direction they wanted to go. It looked like a lot of work for them just to keep up with us, since the snow, even in our snowshoe prints, came up to above their knees. I suppose they could have gone off on their own, but I'd learned from the night before that their stove wasn't working and they didn't have any food beyond a frozen Snickers bar or two, or any water. Without snowshoes to hike fast or a shovel to build a shelter—or a better sense of direction—they were largely dependent on us.

After about fifteen minutes the rocks ran out, but we continued walking downhill anyway. We began thinking that we were too far to the east. The wind was so strong that we were knocked over by the bigger gusts, and we felt it was blowing us off course. We compensated by side-hilling for a ways to the west and then continuing down again, only to think we'd gone too far west, and so we angled back to the east. The problem was, we never seemed to get any lower. After innumerable hours of zigzagging we started finding hills, huge uphill sections, when our route should have taken us straight back down to the Paradise parking lot. We'd crest a hill after what seemed like hours of trudging, only to go down the other side and find another hill after it. We were still far above tree line, and it was snowing sideways so hard we could barely make out each other's shapes as we walked.

We were exhausted and soaked to the skin. My down jacket hung on me like a wet, oversized rag. Water was running down the back of my legs under my rain pants. I didn't have a bit of dry clothing in my pack. My one gear success was the pair of Ed Viesturs-recommended eight-thousand-meter synthetic mittens, so I could still feel my fingers even though they were cold. Everyone else was complaining bitterly that they hadn't been able to feel their fingers or toes for hours.

Finally, it started getting dark and we had to concede we were not going to get out. We decided to dig a snow cave, no matter how long it took, and started taking turns with the shovel. It was impossible going. The snow on the surface was hopelessly soft and loose, and below that was rock-hard ice. We had to switch to chiseling with Steve's ice ax almost immediately.

After five minutes of standing still, Cicily started crying quietly. She was really cold, and said she knew she was going to die there. She refused to dig, and lay down in the snow in a ball. I didn't comfort her. I didn't know how. I'd mostly climbed with guys and Alice, and I'd never had a partner do this before. I reasoned that guys usually wanted space when they had a breakdown so they wouldn't feel embarrassed. I thought that if I left her alone she'd eventually come to her senses and realize that we needed to keep working on this snow cave in order to warm up.

The three of us continued digging in turns. Hours passed. Steve and I were zoning out in our misery, staring into the darkness, and we both started thinking it was strange that Kim had been digging so long, since his turns had been fairly short up to this point. We turned around and found him curled up in a ball inside the tiny shelter, out of the wind. We pulled him out by his ankles and then Steve and I took turns digging. Finally, we couldn't dig any more and we all piled in.

The snow cave was T-shaped, and the guys' side was almost long enough for them to stretch out, but our side had hit impenetrable ice and was only long enough for us to lay on our backs with our knees up to our chests. Both sides were very narrow, and once we'd all gotten in I was basically lying on top of Cicily. Cicily lay there a minute and then screamed at the top of her lungs into the pitch darkness, "I feel very uncomfortable with this situation!" She was crying again and it pissed me off, since there was obviously nothing more I could do. It didn't bode well for our Denali trip. She started sobbing and yelling, "Get off me!"

I had been happy for the warmth, and willing to accept the discomfort in exchange for gaining camaraderie, but Cicily's reaction felt like a denial of all that our friendship could be. It hurt me deeply and made the physical torture all the worse because I knew I was experiencing it for nothing.

"I'll be right back," I said as I wormed my way out of the snow cave, not caring for the moment if I froze to death. No one was going to see how much this final loss had hurt me. I didn't know what else to do for Cicily, but I tried desperately to think of something. I stood there, feeling any remaining heat being blasted away by the mad winds tearing through my wet clothes. I couldn't see anything, and I knew I would die if I stayed out in this for even five more minutes.

I tried feeling my way back into the snow cave, but there was a backpack wedged into my spot. I started to pull it out, but heard Kim's voice, quiet but firm: "This has become a life or death situation and it's everybody for themselves. I need my pack to stay dry." There were no other sounds from within the snow cave. I recoiled, thinking of Scott's race to the Pole, and how Oates had at least been able to decide to die of his own volition.

Back out in the ice shrapnel I reviewed my options. I couldn't leave them and I couldn't stay in the snow cave. I knew digging another cave for myself would take too long. My long underwear was wet, and the next few layers were stiff with ice—my down jacket could have stood up on its own. I'd tried pulling my sleeping bag out of my pack earlier, but it had frozen into the shape, weight, and consistency of a frozen turkey. I'd been unable to massage it into something I could get into, and I knew it would be totally worthless either for warmth or as a wind block. I began feeling that the rest of the evening was going to sort of suck.

Just then there was a light from behind me, and I recognized Steve emerging from the snow cave. He walked over to me and shouted, "I couldn't stay in there anymore." I nodded, immediately and intensely grateful. "We need those bivy sacks," he yelled. After a little investigation I found out that Cicily wasn't even using hers. I'm not sure what Steve said to Kim to get him to give up his.

The wind threatened to pull the bivy sack out of my grasp. It took everything I had to concentrate on pinching it between my two frozen hands. I stuck it over my head and spent a few minutes pulling it down, until my head was at the foot end of the yellow bag and only my feet were sticking out the bottom. It was a relief to be out of the wind, but the ice-encrusted bag was still slapping me in the face, and snow was billowing in from between my feet. I sat down on my backpack with my back to the wind, sitting on my hands because my gloves were so thick I figured they could double as a sit-pad. I leaned forward until my head was on my knees, with one cheek on the crusty fabric, and after a few more minutes of full-body shivering I realized that the muscles in my back and legs had become rigid. I was unable to sit back up.

I spent the endless night shivering violently with my head-lamp on. I was afraid to turn it off, even though I knew I needed to save the batteries—but total darkness added a surreal element that I couldn't bring myself to appreciate. I hadn't been able to feel my toes all day, but there was no way I was going to take my boots off to see what they looked like. Thanks to the mitts I could still feel my fingers, but I had to wiggle them constantly, which was OK since it gave me something to do.

In the morning, just before dawn, the weather wasn't any bet-ter. It had snowed several feet overnight and the wind was still blow-ing the snow sideways, creating huge drifts. Cicily and Kim hadn't tried to dig out the entrance to their cave at all, so they were bur-ied in new snow. My first awareness of life outside the bivy sack—beyond my attempts to sing myself a song, and my irritation at being unable to remember any lyrics, or to concentrate on any thought whatsoever—was muffled screaming coming from the snow cave. It was both a relief and a new agony to take off the bivy sack, and be exposed and free in the storm again.

I stumbled over Steve, who was lying down completely cov-ered in snow, and for a moment I thought he had frozen. It was an enormous relief when he moved slightly and I yelled down at him, "Rise and shine."

It took us a few minutes of digging to locate the snow cave entrance and pull Cicily's pack out. Kim and Cicily piled out after it, sputtering and hysterical. Cicily told me later she had woken up disoriented, or had just become increasingly aware that the snow cave was super stuffy and totally dark. She and Kim had panicked, and pandemonium had ensued. They were tangled in the dark, screaming, until we shoveled them out. It sounded horrible and claustrophobic, and actually made me glad I'd spent the night out.

Cicily's fingertips were black and horrifically swollen. So were Kim's. Steve's left thumb had swelled and darkened so badly that the flesh was split down the side of the nail and the bone was exposed. I was shocked. It was the first time I'd seen bad frostbite in real life. I'd experienced waxen fingertips and the screaming barfies, that condition where the pain of blood returning to your frozen fingers makes you want to scream and vomit at the same time. I'd gotten blisters from ice climbing a few times. But I'd never seen anything that I knew, without a doubt, needed to be amputated. I'd been worried about hypothermia, but I hadn't even considered frostbite. I had thought we'd all get out, warm up, and be fine in twenty minutes, without any negative lasting consequences. Suddenly I realized it wasn't going to work out that way.

I duct-taped a gauze pad loosely around Steve's thumb to keep the skin from hanging down off the bone and looking gross. Cicily wanted me to switch gloves with her since hers were inadequate and soaked, and she knew her fingers were only going to get worse. I wanted to extend an offer of friendship, to repair our frayed relationship—I was in a position to help her—but I said no to save my own skin. I felt awful. But I rationalized that my hands were now a valuable resource since the others were unable to do any task that required dexterity. Plus, she had health insurance and I didn't.

We could hear avalanches going off all around us. We didn't know what kind of slope we were on or what was above us, since we couldn't see any farther than each other. We figured that we probably weren't in the best spot.

I started packing up. I wanted to be as helpful as I could, to justify the gloves decision, so I packed everything and re-laced everybody's boots. Cicily had to use the bathroom and I helped her take her pants off and then put them back on again. She had left her snowshoes flat in the snow the night before, and they'd been covered completely. I looked for a long time, but I could only find one of them.

We started down, but the slope was too steep. We were up to our waists in the snow but falling forward. We didn't remember any place so steep on the snowfield. After about ten minutes we unanimously decided to turn around and wait until we had better visibility before continuing. We were afraid we were above a cliff, and if the slope got any steeper we would slide off. Even if we did come to a cliff and managed not to fall off it, we wouldn't have the strength to hike back up the hill. Swimming in the snowdrifts back up the steep terrain we'd just slid down took us several hours, and we were unspeakably relieved and exhausted once we reached the cave again.

I decided it was time to start cooking. I had tons of food since we'd been planning to stay at Camp Muir for several days, and we hadn't eaten or drunk anything since we'd left Paradise two days before. The stove wouldn't light in the storm, so I lay flat on my stomach and lit it in the entrance to the snow cave, and started melting snow that I'd chipped off the ceiling. Cicily refused to get back into the snow cave, so Steve put her into her bivy sack outside the entrance. Steve was trying to talk some sense into her, but I couldn't hear what he said. Steve would come over periodically and I could tell he wanted me to understand that Cicily was having a serious problem, one I needed to deal with since I was her friend, but I didn't know what to do. I was doing the best I could. Kim just lay down on the other side of the snow cave and stared blankly at me, which was a little creepy.

I made tea—I had six kinds to choose from—and then I made soup. Cicily had a thermos which I filled with soup and had Steve take to her. The stove wouldn't stay lit, so I had to dismantle it several times. In the end I used parts from both stoves to keep it going. I noticed that no one was very hungry except me. I set out cups of hot tea for Steve and they got cold before he came and got them. Kim wouldn't eat or drink anything. I thought this was totally bizarre, since for me the hot liquid was incredibly restorative. I was still shivering constantly, but I finally had to pee for the first time in two and a half days.

That night the wind was crazy, and I wondered if we would all still be alive in the morning. I was baffled at how the situation had become so serious so quickly. Even why it was so serious was beyond me. I wanted to yell at Cicily to buck up and at the others to try the potato-leek soup. It wasn't half bad. Cicily had been uncommunicative all of the previous day and had refused to get out of her bivy sack. Kim wasn't making much sense and wouldn't wear his gloves. I wasn't sure where Steve was. I wanted to make hot water bottles but I couldn't get the stove to stay lit long enough to melt the ice in the Nalgenes, and we didn't have any that were empty. I stayed where I was next to the stove in the snow cave all night, and nobody said anything. I lit the stove and made drinks every few hours, and dug out the cave entrance, and the rest of the time I shivered in a wet, miserable, solitary ball.

By morning the wind had died down, the clouds had disappeared, and the sun was shining. It was incredible. It was almost warm. I was still shivering, and my jaw was cramped because my teeth had been chattering for so long, but finally the cold wasn't quite so insidious, and I hoped maybe some of our stuff could dry out a little bit in the sun. Just outside our snow cave was a pile of rocks covered in rime ice, and we all stumbled over to sit in the sun. Even Cicily got out of her bivy sack, although we had to help her walk. Then we just sat there a long time.

I wanted to try hiking out, but Cicily and Kim didn't think they'd be able to make it in a day, and no one wanted to try to find a new shelter on the way down. There was only one pair of snowshoes left. I didn't want to leave by myself, even to get help, because no one else was able to light the stove or take care of themselves because of their damaged fingers. So we just sat there in the sun.

We tried calling 911 on Steve's cell phone, but we couldn't get service. I was embarrassed that I needed to be rescued. I'd thought we could pull it off, and now I realized we couldn't. It was a demoralizing moment. I'd just put my application in to be a climbing ranger, and getting lost was a fantastic reason for them not to hire me. So I would be jobless. It didn't look like I was even going to have my all-girls' trip to South America. Probably no one would ever want to climb with me again once they knew how badly I'd screwed up. And I'd be friendless. I hunched lower on my ice-covered rock, glaring out from under my saturated balaclava, blinking in the crack of natural light that kept growing bigger as the wet foam on the top of my ski goggles sagged lower and lower down my nose. Regardless of the consequences, calling for help was the right thing to do.

Steve figured that even though our call for rescue didn't go through, he and Kim were now a day and a half overdue and so someone ought to be looking for them. I made a giant X in the snow with our wands just in case Steve and Kim's absence was important enough that a helicopter would come. We didn't see any.

A little before noon a woman skied into our camp. We just

stared at her. "Are you with the lost guys?" she asked, eyeing Cicily and me.

"Yes," I said. "Probably you mean us, anyway."

"You know the Paradise parking lot is crawling with news crews and people out looking for them," she said, pointing to Steve and Kim.

"No," I replied, "we didn't know that."

"Well," she scoffed, "you ought to tell the Park Service where they are." Her disdain was so tangible I had to wonder what scenario might be going through her head—possibly that this was some sort of mock disappearance we'd staged in order to facilitate an illicit romantic tryst—but I didn't care. We could follow her tracks back to the parking lot. I was excited to get out any way we could, and I hoped the others felt the same way.

"When you ski down, could you mark your route with some of our wands?" I asked. "We'd like to follow your ski tracks out, but I'm not sure we'll get out today, and if it snows again we won't be able to follow you." We gave her the rest of our wands. She said she was too cold to stop so she had to run, but she'd mark the route back to the road and let the Park Service know she'd seen us.

I started packing up. The hope of getting out without spending another night, possibly in another storm, gave me fantastically renewed energy, and I stuffed frozen gear into our backpacks as fast as I could. I didn't want to abandon any camping equipment in case we didn't make it out that day.

While I was packing, another skier came along. This time it was a Park Service employee on his day off, Rich, out for a ski on the Paradise glacier, enjoying a break in the weather. Unlike the first skier, Rich seemed interested in helping us back down the glacier. "Hey," I said, "would you let Cicily snowshoe down with you? She doesn't want to spend another night out and we're not sure we can make it down today without snowshoes." It was a huge relief when he agreed and gave Cicily his spare pair of gloves. I strapped my snowshoes on her feet and gave her my car keys.

"Now," I said, "whatever you do, don't go in an ambulance to the hospital because they'll take you to Tacoma. You want to go to Seattle because they have better facilities to treat frostbite." I said this after remembering that Virginia Mason Hospital in Seattle had a hyperbaric chamber. I told her to wait for me if she could, but if she couldn't wait for me to take my car and I'd find a way to catch up with her later.

The remaining three of us started post-holing along, following the tracks that Rich and Cicily had left in the snow. We never did see any wands. I was paranoid that it would start snowing again. The sun had disappeared as quickly as it had come, and the sky looked ominous. I knew with every fiber of my being that we needed to go as fast as possible.

We were taking turns breaking trail, following the tracks, winding our way between crevasses, as it started snowing again. When Kim dropped to his knees and started crawling forward in the waist-deep snow, I didn't say anything, just pushed him out of the way and continued on.

We didn't say anything for hours and hours until I saw my backpack lying in the snow between the prints ahead of us. I was amazed. I still had Cicily's pack and she had mine, but she hadn't been carrying anything in it, so I couldn't figure out why she'd ditched it. I stopped, picked up my pack—which was expensive—and tried to figure out how to affix it on top of the pack I was already wearing.

The backpack didn't fit well since I was still carrying Cicily's remaining snowshoe. I removed the snowshoe and thought, why am I carrying this? I couldn't think of any great use for it. I couldn't walk with just one snowshoe on, I couldn't eat it, and I couldn't use it for warmth. Briefly, I thought that maybe I didn't want to litter. Then, suddenly, I was angry. Here I was, lost in a midwinter epic and carrying two quarts of frozen-solid contact-lens solution and other people's leftover gear. As a beleaguered traveler, shouldn't I strip down to the bare necessities for survival? (Which for me also meant not losing personal gear I couldn't afford to replace.) I refused to carry the offending snowshoe further. I discus-hucked it into a crevasse—let the world judge as it will—attached the two packs, and continued post-holing toward the parking lot.

It got dark and started snowing heavily again, but we continued pushing through the deep drifts. Once below tree line, the promise of the parking lot was overwhelming. We had to continue. When we were totally exhausted—much more so than we'd been days earlier when we'd said we were totally exhausted—we stumbled into a group of mountain rescue folks. There were tons of them, different groups from different jurisdictions all hiking together. Their headlamps looked like a string of Christmas lights in the dark. They all tried to call in on their radios at the same time to say it was their group that had found us. They had brought snowshoes for us. They threw them in a pile at our feet.

"Our hands are frostbitten," said Steve.

"That totally sucks, dude," said one of the searchers, "but we'll get you fixed up as soon as we get back to the parking lot."

They all nodded and stood, looking at us expectantly. I got down on my knees and started putting the snowshoes on Steve and Kim.

We were back in the parking lot in fifteen minutes. There were news crews everywhere. A couple of green-clad Park Service employees hustled us into a Suburban as people with microphones beat on the windows. They drove us down to Longmire, the park headquarters a half-hour down the road from Paradise. I wanted to take my own car, but I learned that Cicily had taken an ambulance to the hospital in Tacoma with my car keys in her pocket.

We got debriefed by my future boss who wanted to know

where we'd been, how the four of us had found each other in the storm, and any other interesting information we had. We didn't know much. They gave me a free phone call and I called my parents, who didn't know I'd been missing, which made sense since I wasn't supposed to have been home until that night, anyway. My mom asked me to say hi to Cicily for her, and hoped we'd had a nice time.

I sat on the front porch of the Longmire Inn, trying to figure out what to do next. Steve and Kim had driven off to Virginia Mason in Seattle. I had to get to Tacoma to pick up Cicily. My friend Alice was driving from Idaho on her way back from a wilderness EMT class, and she said she'd stop by Mount Rainier on her way home to pick me up. Even better, I found out that Cicily had discarded her coat before she'd gotten in the ambulance, and my keys were in the pocket.

A few hours later Alice showed up and gave me a ride back up to Paradise to get my car. Then we caravanned to Tacoma to pick up Cicily. Cicily had been diagnosed with frostbitten fingers and something resembling trench foot, but they wouldn't keep her for the night. They told her to go home to California and deal with the frostbite there. She needed a bath, she said, but she couldn't wash herself since her fingers were all bandaged up. I begged Alice to take Cicily home with her for the rest of the night, until we could get her on a plane. I have never been so grateful to anyone as I was to Alice when she said yes.

To sum up, I lost nearly twenty pounds in four days from shivering and dehydration. Cicily said the experience, along with the months of bandage-changing that followed, inspired her to become a doctor, which she is now. And somehow I got a job working as a climbing and general high-altitude rescue ranger, starting three months later. Cicily and I never did climb together again.

Though I'd been lost on the mountain, I didn't quietly ask for my resume to be returned. I accepted the park's offer of employment even though I didn't understand at the time why on earth I got it. I even showed up that first day, though I had pretty well convinced myself it was a setup. My appearance led to grave concerns from the rest of the staff and outrage from the lead rangers directly responsible for me. They'd thought they would be getting someone they had groomed for the job and were already friends with, but instead they got a girl they hadn't met until she got herself lost in terrain she should have known like the back of her hand. For me, it was a difficult work environment to come into. But I resolved to try as hard as I could to fulfill my dreams. I would learn the skills I needed, and risk as much as I had.

Lately I've been wondering what I'd have told the *News Tribune* reporter if he'd interviewed me a few years later. During my three seasons at Mount Rainier I learned a lot about mountain climbing and rescues, about politics and camaraderie in the mountains, and about what being a woman climber means. Now I know in all certainty when to bring my toothbrush and when to leave it at home and, all things considered, that kind of confidence is hard to come by. The greatest skill I ever had, though, was the one I started with: being able to suffer for long periods of time and not die. In exchange, I got to see some amazing things.

Four days in a whiteout was the beginning of my relationship with Mount Rainier, and what follows are stories of my subsequent work there in my third year as a ranger, my days and nights, and heart and soul. This is my last year on the mountain.

2

THE BOLD AND THE BALLSY

MIKE, OR "GATOR" TO HIS FRIENDS, supervised eleven climbing rangers at Mount Rainier. Two of them were middle-management guys, Glenn and Stefan, who got out on the mountain sometimes but were mostly stuck with office work. Four were the team leaders: David and Chris, with grunt rangers Stoney and Jeremy on the north side; and Charlie and Andy, with grunt rangers Matt and me, Bree, on the south. Adrienne—the other girl who had also decided to stay—and I weren't allowed to work on the same team in the best of times, but she'd injured herself just before the season started and spent the summer out of the field, running the Climbing Information Center. That sounds like a lot of rangers, but it wasn't. Of the eight paid climbing rangers who typically worked on the mountain, on any given day half were having their days off. That left just four rangers to cover the whole mountain, north and south. I worked on the south side, and it was just Charlie, me, and our volunteer, Tom.

When Mike hired me, he said he was collecting eclectic personalities more than anything. He wanted the bold, ballsy, and elite climbing attitude to shine through the government red tape. I think he considered this the last hope of being able do rescues the right way—with a group of people who wouldn't ask permission or give up control over something they knew best about. However, the negative aspects, the intolerance, egomania, and "lone wolf" attitude that came with this personality type, were hard to integrate with the customer-service role of being a climbing ranger, and led to many awkward situations involving offensive language, uniform requirements, substance and beverage regulations, and sometimes a lack of human decency. Mike wanted showy, so while I tried to be a sweetheart on the mountain, I didn't when I was around Mike. When I got hired, we shook hands. "Call me Mike," he said.

The north side rangers were fantastically good rescue rangers, but often so hard to get along with that Mike would sit down and lecture us south side rangers about damage control etiquette. It was up to us, he would say, to be professional and get along with the rest of the park by setting a consummate example of what the park means: uniformed, friendly, and well-mannered. The paradox was that if we succeeded, it meant we weren't good climbers and subsequently weren't his first choice for rescues; and if we didn't, then we weren't doing our part for the team. Sometimes it made me angry, but most jobs have their share of strange politics, and this didn't seem so different from anywhere else.

In October, almost two months after the end of my second season with the park, Mike called me at home. He needed to get a dead guy off the mountain, and no other rangers were around, so he'd had to call me and Adrienne, the girls. "OK," I said flatly, "I'll do it." I'd been waiting two full seasons to play a central part in a rescue, the most important aspect of what a climbing ranger does.

Agonizing flashbacks raced through my mind. All the times I'd been in the right place at the right time to help with a rescue, but Mike had called the north side rangers to drive around the mountain, or he'd recruited someone else during their days off. Worse, he'd call me back to work for rescues during my days off, saying he was desperate for more help. I'd made the three-hour commute from Seattle, but when I got to the park he'd asked me to backfill Camp Muir, or staff the office so we could keep selling permits.

At the start of a rescue, all the climbing rangers would meet in the Park Service's equivalent of a war room in Longmire, but I never got to sit in on those sessions at which everybody else learned where they were going and what the story was. Beforehand, Mike would ask me to make coffee and then he'd ask me to leave when the meeting started, with everybody else staring at me as I left. Then Mike would ask whoever was nearest the door to shut it. I'd stand for a minute alone in the hallway, staring at the wall, before driving up the hill to Paradise.

I never understood why he ousted me from planning meetings. Maybe it fostered some solidarity among those who stayed. I figured it must make the rest of the team stronger, to know they were chosen, even if it was at my expense. I'd spend those days fuming, not understanding why I kept up my emergency medical technician's license and went to rigging and helicopter classes. Some of the other climbing rangers hadn't been current for years, but they had more field experience, and they always would if I never got to do rescues. I shook with fury and found myself overcome with the fear that I was totally worthless, but I smiled when tourists drove up to the ranger station and honked until I came out.

"Is this it?" they'd ask, peering at the fog. Trying to see the mountain behind it.

"Yep," I'd reply, "this is all there is here for us today."

Disappointed, they'd screech out of the parking lot without even getting out of the car.

In retrospect, I wonder that I didn't enjoy those days more. I think I was focused on participating in the human element, striving to have a role in someone else's life and death struggle. And

I thought that to go on a rescue would generate the camaraderie and respect I wanted to share with my coworkers—one of the reasons I'd become a climbing ranger in the first place. This obsession with being left out of rescues blinded me to the amazing things I did have: the wonder of being enveloped and held in the swirling fog, seeing the rain pelting on window panes, the peace of being alone.

But that October when Mike called, I felt that this was my chance at last. It was going to be a difficult assignment. Not particularly time-sensitive (since the man was already dead) and I was already familiar with the terrain, but Mike said he was coming with us and that meant that I was going to have to put on a good show as well as do the actual work.

Unwilling to say no, I drove back to the park from Seattle.

"I can't believe I came back again," said Adrienne, staring around the nearly deserted parking lot when we met at Longmire. In contrast to the dour wintry surroundings, Adrienne looked pissed at herself but vibrant, very blond with her hair in two braids down her back, her nose sunburnt.

"I know," I said numbly, "I shouldn't have come back either."

At that moment Mike came tearing out of the administration building, saw us, and yelled, "Get your packs, we're going to Kautz and we're flying out of here!" He jumped into his van and squealed out of the lot, the engine laboring, towards the Kautz helicopter base fifteen minutes down the road.

We stood where we were and watched the rear of the minivan disappear over the crest of the hill. "I didn't even pack my pack," Adrienne said, "I just threw everything in the back of my truck. I didn't figure I'd actually end up doing anything."

"Neither did I. Let's give it a minute before we follow him."

Half an hour later we were flying over the mountain in a small helicopter, following footprints in the snow. Apparently, as Mike told us the story over the intercom, two men in their early twenties had been caught in an avalanche the day before yesterday. They'd been planning on climbing the Ingraham Direct, the easiest of the standard winter routes on the mountain's south side, and had been holed up at Camp Muir waiting for the weather to clear. Unfortunately for them, the weather never did clear and the snow kept piling up. After a few stiff, cold, and bored days in the public shelter, they'd decided to hike around the area for a bit.

The avalanche buried them as they tried climbing a steep chute above a crevasse. A thick slab of snow broke off from the top of the chute and carried the climbers down into the crevasse with it, crushing them against the frozen crevasse walls. One of the men survived the fall and was able to dig himself out. He attempted to rescue the other man, but it was quickly evident that his friend was already dead.

After climbing out of the crevasse, the surviving man hiked back down to Camp Muir and called the park using the emergency radio in the public shelter. The park's communication center told him to keep hiking down to Paradise, where a law enforcement ranger would meet him, and that they'd send someone up to get his dead friend right away. In reality, though, Mike had had to wait until the weather improved before going up for the body. The dead man's friend was waiting in Mike's office, restless and bleary-eyed after days of inaction and sleepless nights full of regretful reliving, which was why Mike had met us outside.

There was a lot of new snow over the two men's tracks, but the wind had made weird mounds where the steps had been, so from the air we could still tell, sometimes, which direction the climbers had been headed. Then we flew over a place where the two sets of tracks ended and one started wandering separately back down the mountain. We landed as close to it as we could. We pulled our packs out after us and knelt down, huddled over our gear, as the rotors blew the light, unconsolidated snow in our ears, up our noses, and down our shirts.

Suddenly I didn't want to be here, high on the mountain with my boss. I wasn't sure I had accumulated enough inner resources to handle this situation calmly, with the poise, efficiency, and panache Mike would expect. I shut my eyes, clicked my heels together three times, and wished to be back in Kansas—or anywhere else—as Mike threw himself on top of me to protect me from the rotorwash.

When the bird was gone it was suddenly quiet. The snow sparkled in the sun and the cold. We were high up on the mountain, the three of us together, alone with our thoughts. I thought about how we would do this job if it were just Adrienne and me. Probably we would banter about how our winter plans were going, hiking at a reasonable pace to the spot. Then we would remove this man from the mountain with as much respect as we could, and would go for beers and talk about it afterwards. We'd talk about how we were an important part of this man's death, and what it felt like to be part of a death. But we were playing by different rules with Mike here: we weren't good people, we were good climbing rangers.

We sank into the new snow to above our knees. Mike asked me to lead the way uphill. I sort of knew this was coming, since the previous year one of the north side rangers had told Mike I was a great pack animal, not really fast, but able to carry heavy loads over long distances. He said this after I had lugged a pack with close to a hundred pounds of climbing hardware from Ipsut Creek up sixty-five hundred vertical feet to the base of the Willis Wall supporting a rescue on Liberty Ridge, then asked if I could keep going. While I was grateful for the compliment, and its implication that I was in fact useful, I was also worried because I knew Mike wanted to see for himself. In all the time I'd worked in the park we had never before climbed or done a rescue together. In fact, I had never done a climb or rescue with Glenn or Stefan, the next level of management down, either. Mike worked mostly in his office in Longmire, and when he climbed it was with the north side rangers or with special guests like the president of REI, or U.S. senators. It's hard work to make the steps, forcing first one foot and then the other through the snow and ice, crashing down until your feet finally find a layer that supports your weight, and working your way uphill.

Normally post-holing isn't so bad; it's slow, hot work, and team members trade off frequently. But on this trip I knew there would be no switching off. I needed to appear to do this effortlessly, because this would be the only time I would ever hike with Mike. This was how he would always remember me. Until this point, the only comments I'd gotten from Mike during reviews were that he'd like my niche to be dealing with our outdated computer system. The fact that my future doing a real climbing ranger's job depended on how fast I could hike uphill to find a guy who was already dead was nauseating in its pointlessness. I didn't understand why it couldn't be some other way, friendly and companionable.

The temperature was probably less than ten degrees, but I started off in just a T-shirt, knowing I would warm up fast. I wasn't acclimated to the altitude, going from sea level to twelve thousand feet in five minutes. My throat immediately burned and my legs went numb, my vision blurred. The terrain was steeper than I'd remembered. But it didn't matter. I was being good today; I wasn't going to stop no matter what happened. In the frozen silence I could hear Mike and Adrienne breathing ten and twenty meters behind me on the rope we were all evenly tied into. I wondered if they could hear me huffing and puffing, and I tried to breathe quieter. I just had to get through this day, to prove I could not only do my job competently, but in the style Mike wanted to see.

The middle of the glacier was broken, and we spent a lot of

time climbing on and off, over and around the giant blue ice cubes that blocked our way. Finally, after an hour or two, when we knew we were close, we got to the edge of a crevasse that was probably fifty feet across, with a thin ceiling of blue ice and a false floor of jumbled snow blocks creating a sort of tunnel that sagged below the level of the glacier. We were at one end of the narrow opening and we left our packs there, bringing just a rope, a body bag, and a shovel with us. Then we crawled across the false floor, trying to step on the tops of the biggest snow blobs. Every once in a while we could hear pieces falling out from underneath us, creaking off and then slamming against other nebulous things in the bowels of the crevasse. I wondered if the whole floor would collapse under our weight.

We could see light on the other end of the crevasse, and we followed the footprints across the tunnel. On the far side a green wall rose up, angled against a sixty-degree snowslope. Where the two came together, there was a purple head sticking out of the snow, mouth open, looking at us.

"There he is," I said as brightly as I could while my stomach recoiled.

"Oh yeah," said Mike, "looks like him."

Mike tilted his head sideways, as if it made the purple head look more normal. Adrienne was standing behind me, just looking at the head. I wasn't sure if she'd ever seen a dead person before. I didn't think so.

"What's his name?" I asked Mike. I was trying to figure out whether, minus the purple, and the rent in the side of his head, he looked like someone I knew.

"Uh," said Mike, trying to remember.

I realized I did know him. He'd been a volunteer at a fire station I'd been at for a few weeks the previous year while doing a rotation for paramedic school. I also realized I couldn't let Mike know I knew him—I was worried that if I did, Mike would think I'd lose it. I knew I'd see myself as a callous person for the rest of my life for what I was about to do. In order to gain my boss's respect, I was going to lose my respect for myself.

I was soaked from the sweat I'd generated on the climb up, and now in the shade of the crevasse the sweat was freezing and I was shivering. I hoped Mike wouldn't notice—I didn't want him to think I was shivering because I was scared.

"Hey, Mike, throw me that shovel, and I'll try to get an idea of what position he's in."

I started in behind the dead man, at the back of his neck, working my way down. I tried to be careful to dig close but not too close to him, but the snow was very compact and difficult to dig, so every once in a while I would nick the back of his collar or tink him on the head, and it made me cringe. He wasn't frozen really, just stiff, I could tell by the sound. I didn't slow down. I was supposed to be good at this. This was my job.

Mike and Adrienne were taking turns, digging with their hands in front of his head. He looked like he was sitting up, which meant we were going to have to dig a long ways to extricate him from his cramped tomb between the ice wall and the steep snow slope. The rope was tangled around the body and anchored deep below him in the snow, and his pack was mostly buried.

Once we finally got down to his torso, Mike sent Adrienne back across the crevasse to get a knife so we could cut the rope and pack off him. I looked at the dead man's face again—there was red foam bubbling out of his mouth, though he'd been dead for a few days. I remembered that he was twenty-one, gregarious, had a blond Mohawk. He did a lot with his church, was outspoken about it. We'd eaten Thanksgiving dinner together.

Adrienne came back and then we cut the pack straps and the rope, finally succeeding in getting his top half free of the ice. His legs were next, and I found myself looking at them. He had expensive climbing pants. I wondered what would happen to them, if his parents would sell them or burn them. Dead man's pants. I had an introspective moment thinking about how meaningless things take on so much significance after their owner has died. Mike saw me staring at his pants, and there was a momentary pause where I felt sure he was sniffing out weakness in me. Probably thinking I wasn't able to stay in the moment and get the job done in a timely manner without getting mushy. Here the roof could collapse on us, the floor could give way, there could be another avalanche and we'd be smothered, but I was too concerned with the dead guy to be able to prioritize properly.

"Anybody want some M&Ms?" I asked, jerking up, smiling as I pulled the brown packet out of my pocket. "I'm starving." Mike held out his hand greedily, and I ate a few to show I could eat over a dead body. Adrienne shook her head. It was a good move on my part. Showed I wasn't getting mushy.

We had to take the man's crampons off so they wouldn't rip holes in the body bag. When he was finally totally free his left arm stuck straight out and wouldn't fit in the bag. There was only one solution. I leaned on it until something snapped under my weight and I fell over, face first, on the body. Still lying on the body, I winked at Mike. I could feel the dead man's bony hip under me and felt the slight give to his stomach when I pressed on it to get back up. Mike gave me a "you're so sexy" look. The dead man fit in the bag just fine after that. I apologized silently for trying to make everything work out for the living, namely me, at his expense and hoped the dead man would understand.

We lowered him down, hand over hand, back into the crevasse. He was heavy and the bag slid everywhere but the path we wanted it to follow. We didn't dare carry him because we weren't sure the false floor would hold all our weight. At the same time, we didn't want to just let go and have him slide to the far corner of the crevasse, where there was a huge hole in the floor. If he slid through that, he'd plummet to the bottom of the glacier and disappear. Eventually, we couldn't hold the body bag anymore and we let it go free. It slid down the icy slope, slamming into the wall at the bottom before, thankfully, lodging itself against a big snow blob a dozen feet away from the hole.

Dragging him up the other side of the crevasse was even more difficult. I clung to the body bag by the front handles, heaving him up in spurts of exertion. Adrienne sat at the far edge of the crevasse and hand-over-handed the slack, while Mike walked down the slope with the rope over his shoulder, trying to keep tension. There were a few news helicopters flying above and we had to stage the body at the edge of the crevasse, just under its roof, out of view of their cameras.

We called our helicopter back, telling the pilot to bring a thick cable that attaches under its belly with a hook on the end. When it came we enmeshed the body in a net and hooked it to the helicopter, and it flew off, swinging, back down to Kautz where the friend could identify it for the coroner. The family could come stand in the middle of the green airfield and cry, or pray, or do whatever they wanted for a few minutes, before they'd be escorted away, maybe even before we got back.

We sat there on our packs for a bit. It was really nice just to sit in the sun, not moving, but the silence was getting awkward. Mike was fidgeting and I worried about our inability to carry on an easy conversation. We weren't good enough friends to weather long silences, and I feared the silence was proof of my failure to entertain. Mike looked bored—bored with us. "So," I said, "I used to know that guy." Mike and Adrienne looked at me. "He was a volunteer fire fighter at a station I was at for a while."

"Really?" Adrienne looked shocked.

"Yeah," I reminisced in a jovial tone of voice. "He was a Republican, right-wing, evangelical Christian. Good fucking riddance he's dead, really." Mike laughed so hard he fell off his backpack into the snow, tears coming out his eyes. I was immediately disgusted with myself. But I started counting on my fingers while Mike brushed the snow off his back. If I got rehired it would only be a few more months before I'd get to do this every day. Well, if I was lucky. If this was lucky.

3

DEAD MEN AND DUST MOTES

WHEN I STARTED WORK AT THE END OF APRIL, it was shaping up to be the most prolific rescue season anyone could remember. Besides the dead man in the crevasse the previous October, the winter had seen several other incidents. Then two Rainier Mountaineering guides were rescued after becoming disoriented in a horrendous storm. Having climbed Ptarmigan Ridge, they'd ended up descending some combination of Gibralter Ledges and the Nisqually Ice Cliff in early February.

My first week back was strenuous but uneventful. There was the first summit climb of the season, which always seemed to be the hardest. I did a good deal of skiing during which I managed one really impressive fall. I filled out all my forms for housing, keys, uniforms, radios, batteries, radio chargers, radio holders, badges, and nametags. I cleaned the mouse turds off every surface in my assigned room in the ski lodge at Paradise and spent hours on the phone with the maintenance division, trying to come up with a noninvasive way to deal wit the stinky and seemingly nocturnal family of woodpeckers that had had nested in the wall next to my bed. On their suggestion I opened the window next to the hole and banged on the wall, and the birds and I would both stick our heads out and try to glare each other down. I blinked, they won. I told myself I could get used to the smell.

Then in the first week of May there was another storm on the mountain. I spent my days off lying inert on a friend's couch in Seattle, watching the rain and reruns of *Murder, She Wrote*. Ted, Rich's employee and the park's maintenance division expert on servicing solar dehydrating toilets, was up at Muir. I think Ted might have been in his sixties. From Thursday to Sunday in the summers, he stayed at Muir as the official "turd herder," cleaning the bathrooms and doing small maintenance jobs. He had a fuzzy gray comb-over and crooked yellow teeth. The eight-by-twelve-foot hut was always strewn with his dozen or so pairs of cheap reading glasses, all of them broken in one way or another, and his books, warped from the humidity: *Egyptian Hieroglyphics Uncovered*, a biography of Napoléon Bonaparte written in French, maps of the Inside Passage, a coffee-table book of green fields in Ireland. I'm not convinced Ted knows French.

Ted told me later that during that storm there was a mound of snow several feet high inside the door of the hut where the spindrift had blown in around the edges and through the cracks and air holes in the walls. Every time he went out, he had to beat on the door until the ice seal broke, and yank on the tiny loose kitchen cabinet handle until the door swung inward. When he looked out, he realized the snow reached to the top of the door frame in a white wall. When he touched it, it spilled inwards over everything. Spindrift blew in his eyes and ran down his shirt and into his boots and his ears. He had to swim his way out. Inside the hut, everything was damp and foggy and freezing. When he used the stove to make dinner—the same meal he made every night, basmati rice with tuna and Popeye canned spinach on top—the heat of the stove melted all the snow in the tiny plywood hut, which later refroze into a layer of sheet ice covering everything.

Ted had been drinking tea when Mike showed up. I always liked to hear the details of Ted's stories, and I pictured him drinking out of his one huge plastic mug with four Lipton tea bags and four sugar packets while lying on the back bunk in his long underwear and his gray socks with the red toes, the same as always. Ted liked his routines. Mike had snowshoed up to the hut so he could snowboard back down from Camp Muir, which is nothing more than a group of tiny huts perched on a rock outcrop at ten thousand feet. Mike had passed a few people on the way up, but he thought they would turn around because of the weather. Ted offered him some tea before he headed back down.

I like storms. I like the energy, the overpowering and irrational force of them. There are so few opportunities to experience that kind of honest upfront and unfocused passion, elemental suffering. I like it when the wind blows the snow so hard that ice shrapnel tears into my face, strong enough to cut the exposed skin on my cheeks. I like it when I can lean against the wind, and the wind slowly blows me backwards, ripping at my clothes until I'm forced to drop to my stomach and crawl. I like skiing when I can't tell if I'm going right or left, up or down, if I'm about to hit something, or even if I'm moving at all. The danger and frenetic nature of the thing inspires madness, and this was that sort of storm.

I had to start work at six the morning after the storm, so I left Seattle at three AM. The rain had stopped, the storm was over, and a crescent moon was showing through a hole in the clouds. I was feeling refreshed after my days of lethargy on the couch, and was ready to face whatever was coming to me.

I stopped for groceries, loading up with almost two hundred dollars' worth. Working a seasonal job with no permanent home elsewhere, I started from scratch every year, re-buying the staples, the peanut butter, flour, pancake mix, syrup, condiments, spices, tea, sugar, brownie mix, rice, cans of things, anything that would be too much of a pain to carry around in the trunk of my car during the off-season. I didn't use a shopping list, relying instead on impulse. This time I decided to go for sixteen boxes of macaroni and cheese, among other things. I paid up and wheeled my cart back to my car, the only one left in the lot.

It was still dark. I put the groceries in the car, got in and turned the heat all the way up, though I knew it would make me drowsy. It's hard not to fall asleep on the way to the park, but I hogged the heat, driving with my wrists on the wheel and one hand in front of each vent, loving every last second of being warm. The last forty minutes inside the park boundary were the hardest. The road is tricky. It lets you drive sixty for a while and then throws a series of ten-mile-per-hour U-turns at you right when you get comfortable. It's also perennially foggy. It was especially foggy that morning, because it was warming up after the storm. The last of the snow on the road was melting. With the slush and the fog I drove slowly, peering out, alternating one eye open, then the other, since they refused to both stay open at the same time.

I got to Paradise at quarter to six, at dawn, but I didn't really notice. My head was in its own fog from the early morning and the recent loss of the car interior's coziness. I carried all my groceries in one trip up the three flights of stairs to my room, the plastic bag straps cutting into my wrists. I had fifteen more minutes to sleep. My bed was Park Service-issue, a twin with a lumpy mattress and stripped bolts holding the frame together. I had to get in carefully because it rocked wildly back and forth, threatening to collapse entirely when I weighted it. I didn't even take my shoes off, just set my alarm, brushed off the fresh mouse droppings, and eased in.

I got up fifteen minutes later and changed into my uniform, the green polyester pants that are too tight around my thighs, two T-shirts for warmth, and my Park Service shirt and fleece jacket,

both with matching official badges. I made a cup of tea to comple-
ment the pumpkin muffin I'd picked up at the grocery store, and
then walked over to the Climbing Information Center.

It was a slow day, sunny but with few people despite the
improving weather. Between issuing climbing permits and talking with the tourists who were mildly interested in climbing the
mountain—but who never would—I had time to clean the bathroom and drag each one of the giant cheap floor mats down the
stairs and out the back door so I could beat them with a broom
I'd borrowed from the public restroom utility closet. When I was
done with the domestic work, I sat on a stool behind the long front
desk and watched the dust motes in the afternoon sunshine until
three o'clock, when we closed.

I had just locked the door when Mike called to say that there
were two people missing on the mountain, and could I find them
in the computer registration system. It wasn't an unusual request.
Almost every day an issue comes up with a climbing party. Sometimes there is a legitimate problem and the missing people are
late because of bad weather but are managing to work their way
down slowly, or else they're lost, exhausted, or dead. But most of
the time they've just decided to stay an extra day or two without
telling anybody, and all that's required is a quick radio call to the
ranger at Muir to go root them out of their tents and send them
on their way. Sometimes it's a little more complicated, like when
a worried wife calls to confirm the dates of her husband's trip, but
we have no record of him.

As a safety net, the day after a party is supposed to be off
the mountain, their party name pops up automatically on the
computer screen, along with their license plate number. I take
this information down and then walk through the parking lots,
row by row. If the car isn't there it's assumed the party has just
forgotten to check out, and I erase them from the computer

system. If the car is still there, I call Camp Muir and see if someone up there can check for them. This time, though, there was no one at Muir to call: Ted had come down on Monday. It was now Wednesday, and no one had replaced him yet. I pulled up the party name Mike gave me, got the license number, and walked through the lot until I found their car. I called Mike back. He asked me to pack and tell Andy to do the same, and come down to Longmire. I said OK, I'd be right there, and then I walked back towards the Paradise dorm. I stopped at the basement window of the Jackson Visitor center, pulled it open a little, and yelled in at Andy, who lived in the rat-infested old law enforcement office. Andy came to the window and said he was making lunch and was going to finish up, do the dishes real quick, and then he'd be ready. We weren't worried about speed because we were rarely asked to actually do anything—the north side rangers did most of the glory jobs.

Twenty minutes later, I drove over to pick Andy up. It's a half-hour ride downhill from Paradise to Longmire. When we got there we waited another couple hours for the north side rangers to drive around from White River. Then I waited outside the administration building, sitting on the edge of its wide concrete porch, for the meeting to finish up, since I'd been asked to leave after making the coffee.

When it was over, Glenn came and told me that Andy and I were going to get on a small helicopter at the Kautz helibase and fly over the mountain to see if we could see anybody. I was a little surprised, but it turned out that David, one of the lead north side rangers, had forgotten his boots and there wasn't enough daylight left for him to drive a couple more hours back to get them. So Mike had gotten pissed and given me his spot. The north side rangers like to work together, because they know they can trust each other, so if I was going, that meant the other spot had just opened up, too.

Flying over the snowfield, on the back bench seat in the helicopter, Andy was looking out one window and I was looking out
the other. We had just flown over the hills below the mountain, my
favorite part of these helicopter rides—the green hills with their
meadows on top looked so green and exotic and remote. I loved it
when the pilots dipped down into the deep gorges at the bases of
melting glaciers. Then, as we got higher, we could see Paradise and
Panorama Point with its paved hiking trails and the famous flowers
that wouldn't bloom for several more months. And then the snowfield, which was really white because of all the fresh snow from
the storm. The mountain was all black rock and snow. I thought it
looked more complicated than beautiful.

We flew up the Nisqually Glacier side, climber's left, slowly
and low, almost in the shadow of the mountain in the late afternoon sunshine. Looking down, everything we saw was white. I
wondered why we were looking for these guys with a helicopter
instead my going on foot, like usual, to check Muir. Why the fuss
this time? I wasn't in the meeting, so I didn't know anything about
the men we were looking for, but I did know that after a big storm,
everybody's late getting out.

I'd heard from Ted that before he'd come down from Muir he'd
talked to a big group of skiers at the Muir shelter, and they'd turned
away two guys at the height of the storm—they'd looked cold and
weren't wearing enough clothing, the skiers said, but there wasn't
enough room for them. According to the skiers, the two men had
a tent, which had probably eased the group's consciences. The two
men had told the skiers that their plan was to head down. Nobody
told them there was a ranger station fifty feet away, where Ted
would have invited them to stay and fed them spinach and rice, and
good conversation. I'm sure, though, that in the blowing snow they
wouldn't have been able to see the tiny hut.

When our helicopter flew over Camp Muir there were ski

tracks, and a few people were walking back and forth below us. Probably clients of the guide service, or part of the ski group Ted had seen. The top and exposed side of the ranger hut glistened, encased in ice a few inches thick, beautiful and classically arctic.

We turned and started back down the snowfield, weaving slightly, looking down over the edge of the snowfield onto the Paradise Glacier, climber's right. We were about twenty-five feet over the snow, and as we dropped down past Anvil Rock I spotted a red backpack. As the pilot swung around I could see the men, about fifty feet apart, both of them lying face up in the snow. We flew in tight circles above them. The wind from the blades blew snow over them and they didn't move—then we knew they were dead. It was fully dusk, the sky was pink and the sun was gone. We had to go back to Kautz because the pilot didn't have instruments to fly in the dark, and we didn't have the equipment to pick the men up.

When we got back to the helibase, David came up to us as we were taking our packs out of the helicopter. "Are you sure they're dead?"

"Yeah, David," Andy replied, looking down. "They're dead."

"Because," David continued, "if they're not dead and you just said they were, then you just killed them, because they won't survive tonight. Think of their families, think of your consciences. How do you know they're dead?"

"Well," said Andy, "we flew right over them and they didn't move, they were being covered in snow and they'd obviously been there a while. If a helicopter flew right over me and I wasn't dead yet, I'd do my best to try to signal it somehow."

"And they didn't," I added. "They didn't move at all. They looked really dead."

David, his wild hair and bushy black beard framing his squinty eyes, didn't reply. He pivoted on one heel and went to talk to Mike. A moment later Mike came over. "Are you sure they're dead?"

"Mike," I asked, "do you want us to hike up there tonight and check for pulses? It was getting dark and we couldn't land there. We were as sure as we could be without being able to land." I paused and looked at Andy, then back to Mike, and said again, "They're dead," firmly and with conviction.

"OK," said Mike. "I'll tell the families."

When I got back to the Paradise dorm I washed out the macaroni and cheese pot I'd used for lunch and refilled it with water for more macaroni and cheese. I vowed I'd cook it until it was actually done, no crunchy noodles this time. I waited an extra five minutes and then added the powdered cheese pouch and sat down at the big communal kitchen table all alone to eat. I noticed we'd caught a mouse in one of our traps. It was dead and there was blood on the floor. I touched it with my shoe; it was stuck to the linoleum. It could have been dead there for days before I'd noticed it. I got up and moved to a chair on the other side of the table where I couldn't see it while I ate.

In the morning, back at Longmire, I sat next to David at the conference room table before the meeting started.

"Y'know, David," I said, "I know you're more experienced at doing rescues and that you can totally do this recovery better than I can, but they're already dead and I could use the experience, and since I started this, I'd like to finish it." I don't know why I wanted to go back there. Maybe I wanted to seem competent enough to do the job, maybe I wanted to make some kind of gesture, something no one else would do, but something that would be meaningful.

He didn't even look at me. "I need the money."

"OK," I said, "I understand that, you know a pint of Ben and Jerry's has gone up to almost four dollars." David looked at me in disgust. He was a vegan. I'd forgotten.

I sat outside during the meeting. Afterwards, Stefan told me to get my pack and go down to Kautz. He and Andy and I were going to do the recovery. I guess David had changed his mind.

Crouched with Andy and Stefan in the snow after the helicopter dropped us off, it was too bright to look at anything without sunglasses: another sunny day, quiet and calm, with at least a foot of new snow covering everything. While I pulled off my flight suit, which involved sitting down and taking my boots off, Stefan pulled out a sandwich. I wished I'd brought one, and I looked over at Andy and saw him eyeing it, too. We sat in silence a minute, both of us watching Stefan chew. Looked like ham and cheese with lettuce and an actual tomato on it. There was nothing to say. After he finished, we left our packs and hiked down towards the place where we had seen the men. We sank into the warm soft snow to above our knees, which made for slow going, but the slope was fairly steep and it wasn't far before we could see them lying down below us.

We got to the first man and I could see that he was old. His hands were covered with age spots and he had a few days' growth of white beard on his cheeks. He was sitting propped up against his backpack with his hands on his knees, staring out across the glacier, although I figure he was probably staring into the darkness when he died. He had light blue eyes and the lids were half-closed like he was thinking about something that was not in the darkness or on the glacier. His headlamp was still on and I reached up and turned it off without thinking—it was wasting the battery. He had on cotton khaki pants that were wet and frozen to his legs, and a wool plaid shirt. A tent was half sticking out of his pack, and all the poles were bent and broken. Half of a blue vintage Eddie Bauer down sleeping bag was pulled out of the pack lid and wrapped down over one shoulder like he had tried to use it for warmth, but hadn't tried very hard. He looked like he had sat down to wait.

Stefan took pictures for the coroner and then drew a sketch

showing where the man was in relation to the rock and the slope. Then he pulled the man's oatmeal-colored wool hat down over his eyes so the dead man wasn't looking at him while he went through his pockets. None of us said anything.

We moved on to the red pack that we'd seen abandoned in the snow. It was an older pack that also looked like it had hurriedly been put back together. Near it we found what looked like a tent platform that had been dug flat in the snow and then abandoned. Stefan took pictures and drew another sketch, and then we walked down further, with each step sinking deeper as the sun rose higher and the snow became softer and wetter.

The second man was very young. Later I found out he'd just gotten engaged. He was skinny and his face was smooth and expressionless. He was lying flat on his back with his hands in the pockets of a thin blue nylon windbreaker. He was wearing shorts and his knees were black with frostbite, even though there were more clothes in his pack. He didn't have a hat, so we used a glove to cover his face. And took more pictures, and did a few more sketches.

I thought they looked like they'd been dead a while. I didn't say anything.

Andy and I started chopping out small platforms under the bodies so that we could get them into body bags and nets to fly out. We wanted to make sure we had a flat spot under each one so that once we started moving him, he wouldn't slide away from us and accelerate down the glacier. The snow was so soft that it didn't take us long to create spaces that were about six feet wide and ten feet long. We were down to our shirtsleeves by the time we'd finished. Then Andy held one of the men under the armpits and I grabbed the ankles. We dislodged him from the slope and slid him down on top of the body bag and open net as best we could, trying to keep as much snow out of the bag as possible. We did the same with the other man. We intended to hook the nets one at a time to a cable that hangs fifty or a hundred feet under the helicopter. In that way we could get them off the mountain quickly and without having to slide them down the main climbers' path in front of whoever might be headed up to Muir that afternoon.

I remembered Glenn telling me about finding two boys who had fallen to their deaths on an icy day a little ways above here, just at the base of the Cleaver. He didn't have any nets or body bags with him, so he had to fly them out with the cable just hooked to their climbing harnesses. He figured that if he flew the dead boys out one at a time, each hanging from his waist and splayed out with his head and arms and legs dangling down, it would look really bad, especially since, because of where the accident had happened, the helicopter would fly right over Camp Muir and all the climbers there. He decided to hook both of the bodies in at the same time and then he duct-taped them together so they'd stay upright, so it looked like they were holding onto each other.

When we finished getting our two men into the bags and the nets, we called the helicopter and then we had a minute to sit down. It was totally silent. Just the intense sunlight and the snow sinking imperceptibly down as it melted. We looked down at Paradise. Andy spoke up.

"I think they decided to set up their tent, but for some reason after they'd set it up they decided to leave again, so they stuffed it all back into their packs. Maybe as they were hiking down they lost each other in the storm, the older guy thought the younger guy was behind him and he sat down to wait. The younger one realized he too was alone and maybe he left his pack in an attempt to go faster but then didn't go more than ten yards past it."

"Hmm," said Stefan. It didn't make much sense to me, them being out here like this, but strange things happen all the time. There was probably something that should be said, I thought, regarding strange things like two men who had died lost alone in the dark and were then found in the brilliant sunshine. But we didn't say anything more. Maybe it was enough to be here and see it.

The helicopter came and we hooked the nets up to it, and it flew off with one man at a time attached to the end of a giant steel hook, a very loud and industrial end considering the men died in a beautiful natural place. After they were both gone we post-holed back up the hill, and I felt the sweat running down my back. Andy and Stefan had been waiting for me for a few minutes by the time I made it back to the packs, trying not to look like I was breathing hard. Then we flew back to Kautz.

Someone had placed the body bags in the shade. We had to walk right by the family, who'd come to identify the bodies, but we didn't talk to them. Didn't look them in the eye. They didn't know who we were and we didn't tell them. Andy and I drove back up to Paradise, and I went back to the dorm. I washed out my cooking pot and put it back on the stove for macaroni and cheese. I ate alone.

Before I was done, Stefan called and asked me to staff the Climbing Information Center for the rest of the day, so I walked over and sat watching filtered sunshine through the windows. It was a slow afternoon.

4

THE COLD HEARTED

BY EARLY JUNE, my routine was falling into place—the trainings, refreshers, and check-ins finally over—and I was looking forward to just doing my job on my next eight-day shift, Wednesday to Wednesday. The first six days were busy but passed without major incident. I post-holed thirty thousand feet uphill, most of it with my ever-present backpack weighed down with vegetables and jars of Nutella as I made trip after trip up to restock Muir. This made the week's three summit climbs from Muir with a light load feel relaxing. Then there were the afternoon hours spent talking to climbers at Muir before their summit bids, some light construction, and the inevitable midnight medical calls. (Climbing rangers are on call twenty-four hours a day, for whatever emergency comes up, though our paid hours are 6:00 AM to 4:30 PM.)

By day seven I found myself staring off into space, unable to focus my eyes or my mind on the simplest of tasks, thoroughly exhausted and ready for my days off. Sometimes being exhausted is a wonderful feeling. There is nothing like being mentally, physically, and emotionally picked clean, not to mention unreasonably dehydrated, battered, and sunburnt—and then being allowed to sleep. That is a kind of sleep like no other, and I was ready for it. But the week wasn't over yet, and I was wary of what might come next.

From my first two seasons on the mountain, I'd learned that climbing rangers don't have breaking points—they don't get tired, or stressed out. They laugh at adversity and always enjoy a fresh challenge. The year before, Charlie and his old lead Paul had climbed Liberty Ridge in a day, carrying over to Camp Muir. As soon as they'd arrived at Muir, Paul had found a large, ill climber and had ended up carrying him piggyback almost all the way down to Paradise. Then at the parking lot Paul had found out the man's partner was missing, and immediately hiked back out to look for him.

I wanted to demonstrate these same abilities, but for some reason I got tired. I wasn't as fast a hiker as the guys, and on a rescue—the most important thing we did—nothing was valued more than foot speed. I was really good at first aid, rigging, general maintenance, assessing the climbing routes, and teaching people about their equipment, park history, and how to keep the mountain clean, but it still took me three hours to get from Muir to the summit, and that meant I wasn't as valuable to the team. The resulting shame weighed me down further.

Anyway, on day seven as I was fantasizing about sleeping a whole night through, Stefan was going stir crazy after having spent all week in his office, and decided that the team—Stefan, Charlie, and I—needed some exercise. So we hiked right back up to Muir in the blazing midday heat in full uniform, since Stefan liked uniforms.

I started out already dehydrated from the week's earlier exploits, and I drank all my water before I was halfway to Muir. My dark green cotton-and-polyester-blend pants were stiff and clinging to my legs, making every step harder. I had to stop at around eight thousand feet. The mountain slowly revolved around me and

I gagged, but there was nothing in my stomach to throw up. While I was bent over, a stinging mixture of sweat and sunscreen trickled into my eyes, blinding me, but I had to keep moving. Stefan and Charlie had gone ahead and were waiting for me at Muir, and they knew what time I'd left the parking lot. I took a few deep breaths and started up again, blinking and weaving. I felt useless, but kept repeating to myself, "You're OK, you're an embarrassment, everything is OK, this is easy, just for god's sake go faster!" Climbing rangers never puke.

Knowing I'd be visible to Stefan and his binoculars five hundred vertical feet before I actually got to Muir, I tried to keep up appearances. That meant no stopping, no faltering, and no heavy breathing. I managed to arrive at Muir with a smile pasted on my face, but I was thankful when the suggested continuation to Ingraham Flats never materialized. Instead we hung around for about an hour, and then I let gravity pull me back down to Paradise.

More than ever I was ready for a full night's sleep, cradling my Camelbak so I wouldn't have to get up when I woke desperate for water every few hours . . . but I didn't get it. Andy called on the dorm's phone at two in the morning, and I jumped out of bed fully clothed. (Something came up almost every night, and I learned I would rather face whatever it was with my pants on. On holidays, weekends, and when I was too tired to take them off, I also wore my shoes.)

Some of the employees at the Inn had been partying outside, complete with drunken dancing, and a girl had fallen off a picnic table and broken her arm. Andy had been rousted by the partyers to drive the girl to the hospital—another part of our job description, midnight hospital runs, with or without an ambulance. Andy and Tom were handling the situation, but they asked me to fill Mike in and to call a private ambulance company to meet him in Ashford, just outside the park, so Andy didn't have to drive all the way to Tacoma.

The phone directory was in the ranger station a quarter mile up the road, so I stumbled down the three flights of stairs and out into the parking lot. As I walked slowly through the dark I could see the lights of the party and hear the music down at the picnic area. I wondered why anyone would be jumping around on picnic tables if they had the option of sleeping instead.

The next morning, I was still bleary-eyed at our yearly wildland fire refresher and physical agility test. Most park rangers moonlight as wildland fire fighters for a little extra money, and I was no exception. The refresher was a long PowerPoint presentation without pictures, and the test was a timed three-mile hike along a flattish dirt road with a forty-five-pound pack. Coming in under forty-five minutes was supposed to indicate that we could outrun a fire uphill, jumping the crest to safety before we got burned over and cooked.

The weather had crapped out and it was drizzling lightly. Everybody was wet and the road was getting muddy. I didn't have enough soup cans to get my pack to the required weight, so I'd had to add some rocks and now the inside of my pack was muddy, too. As I walked, the straps of the ridiculously loaded pack pushed down painfully on my already bruised hips, and I worried about my bad knee. It was sort of funny in a miserable kind of way, a bunch of people in matching uniforms carting cans of soup up and down an old dirt road in the rain, but the money from fire fighting made any training worth it. My mind drifted to more pleasant circumstances as I was swept up into the group of power-walkers.

My days off started officially at four-thirty that afternoon, as soon as this fire test was over. I pictured myself in my car, speeding down the winding road between Paradise and Longmire, my laundry in the back seat, heading towards a sub sandwich and then a pint of Ben & Jerry's ice cream—and then the South Hill Park and

Ride, where I'd lock my car doors and sleep for a long time without anyone knowing where I was.

Stefan jogged up behind me and interrupted my reverie. "Hey, the glaciologists need somebody to help ferry their gear from Camp Muir to Camp Schurman, can you do it?"

"Sure" I said mindlessly, ready to please. "Is the trip next week?"

"Oh," he said, "they're up at Camp Muir right now. They're planning on climbing tonight, but you'll be up there in time to carry their stuff to the summit if you start up right after we're done here."

He slapped the back of my backpack and turned around, jogging the wrong way down the course so he could encourage some of the lady law enforcement rangers to make it across the finish line before the forty-five-minute deadline.

Up until that moment I had been able taste the Ben & Jerry's—it was so close, a miracle of chocolate and marshmallow créme and little smiling, tasty fish. But in a second it was gone, and there was just me in the rain on a muddy road in the woods with a bunch of wet people wearing green, and none of us were going to get any ice cream. It was disappointing, but I had to keep walking with the rocks in my pack for another two miles—and then I would have to keep walking all night.

Being tapped as mule for the glaciologists was actually a favor, because it gave me a chance to show I was useful in some way. At my last season's-end review, Glenn told me that I wasn't a team player, that I didn't have anything special to contribute. I needed a niche, a skill, a special project. I was devastated, thinking I was unlikable and incompetent. But in a lot of ways what he said made sense. I *wasn't* a team player. That year my assigned government housing was in a different zip code from the rest of the climbing rangers who lived, ate, and commuted together. Then when I wasn't alone in Paradise, I was alone at Muir. I'd spent forty days scheduled alone at Muir that summer because, as the others got to know each other, they wanted to climb together, and it became easier for scheduling if I did the opposite assignments so we had good coverage. Even more than the rest of them, I'd never climbed, talked to, or even seen Glenn except for review day, so it made sense that he didn't think I did anything.

This year, though, we all lived together in Paradise and things had gotten friendlier. But there were also fewer of us, to the point where we were almost always on our own, working in the ranger station, staffing Muir, or soloing the mountain. This all meant that when a weird job like helping the glaciologists was offered to me, I had damn well better do it to prove I was worth keeping around.

"I've already hiked over thirty thousand feet this week," I told Charlie back at the dorm, to explain why I was propped up at the kitchen table instead of hiking up the mountain.

"Don't forget to fill out your accountability sheet for what you did this week, on your way up," he said, looking up from scrambling a whole carton of eggs. "You can leave it in my box."

I tried to pull myself together but my body wouldn't respond, it just sat slumped over on a chair. I put my head down on the dining table for a second, and it felt so good to be supported.

I woke up and Charlie was sitting across from me, eating a huge pile of breakfast burritos. One whole side of my face was wet from drooling on the table. My eyes wouldn't focus on Charlie so I looked past him and out the window. It was getting dark. The clouds were thicker and the rain was pelting up off the asphalt in the parking lot. I couldn't see the Tatoosh Range across the valley because it was full of clouds. I could barely see the trees on the sides of the parking lot. Groaning, I wiped the drool off my cheek with the back of my hand.

"You'd better go soon," Charlie said, offering me a burrito.

My clothes were still wet, but it didn't matter. Everything was going to get wet in a minute anyway. I barely brought anything with me, just a map, compass, headlamp, jacket, gloves, and what I was wearing—less than five pounds in all. I figured it was all I was going to be able to carry, and still get there. I rolled my things in a garbage bag to keep them drier and stuffed them into my pack. Everything else I needed for climbing I could get from the gear stash at Muir and from scavenging through Tom and Charlie's plastic storage bins. I knew they had eaten most of my chocolate bars already this season, so I figured I'd return the favor.

Food and equipment was always being accumulated at Muir. For example, over my most recent days off, two men had tried climbing Gibralter Ledges, but at the top one of them had tripped and slid down the forty-five-degree slope, eventually tumbling over a small rock outcropping, and then nine hundred feet further down Gibralter Chute. Andy and Matt had hiked up from Muir and performed CPR for a while, but eventually they'd been forced to leave the body and get the partner out because of bad rock fall. Earlier that morning, Ted had lent the dead man a water bottle. After the partner had retrieved the dead man's belongings, he'd hiked the bottle back up to Ted and thanked him for letting them borrow it. Ted never threw anything away, but he'd said later that he thought it was too weird to drink out of a dead man's bottle so I knew it was still sitting in the corner of the hut.

The rain ran furrows in my hair and spilled like a waterfall into my eyes. The beginnings of these sorts of trips were always the worst for me, while I still remembered what being warm felt like. It was dusk on a Wednesday in the pouring rain and no one was around. The meadows were a blackish green and bone-achingly cold—the bowed, absorbent valerian glowed white in the flat light. The lupine, green hellebore, and few pussytoes bunched in tight to the trail were beautiful, but even they looked vaguely foreboding in the gloom. There weren't any animals out. The giant silverish marmot that lives just below Pan Point didn't even bother to come out and see me. I felt abandoned, imagining him in his burrow under the big rock, cozy and sleeping.

I stopped for a minute at Pebble Creek to get my headlamp out, and was instantly chilled. Every hair on my arms was individually coated in its own layer of hard frost. I didn't put my jacket on. It would have gotten wet, and I needed it to be dry on the upper mountain. The rain had changed to freezing fog and I could tell I was into the clouds now. The fog from my breath completely obscured the way, blocking the light of my headlamp, but the clouds were so thick around me I couldn't tell which way to go anyway. I didn't want to stop and get my compass out—I was worried I would never warm back up again. Instead I went with my gut feeling on the direction and kept walking slowly, sustainably. My legs moved like a metronome.

It was late when I made it above Anvil Rock, a little over halfway to Camp Muir. I could see the outline of the rock in the dark and I realized I was above the clouds. I looked up to see a million stars and no moon. I looked back behind me and saw the gray roll of the fog curling around and caressing the snow in a line that ran across the slope, around the mountain, and then flat in a dark mass covering the earth, running to the horizon line. I was happy to be out of the clouds, but the starry night also chased away my slim hope that bad weather would keep the glaciologists from climbing over to Camp Schurman. The show would have to go on.

When I got to Camp Muir all the lights were out. I looked at my watch. It was ten-thirty. The ranger hut, where the glaciologists were staying, was dark. I knocked lightly, and a man groggily called, "Come in."

"Hi," I whispered, opening the door. "I'm Bree. I'm here to help carry your things over to Camp Schurman."

"Oh, OK. We left you some dinner." There was a pot on the

countertop. I pointed my headlamp and saw about half a cup of phad thai frozen to the bottom of the pot. I ate it in two mouthfuls.

"I'm Jen and this is Rob," said a voice from within the other sleeping bag. Rob was sleeping on the back bunk, and Jen was sleeping on the bunk that folded out from the wall, leaving just enough space for one person to stand sideways between it and the countertop.

"I'm just going to make up my bed," I whispered, scrunching down under Jen's foldout bunk. There was another foldout bunk nobody used because all the rescue gear was hanging off it, and when it augured down the gear jammed against the floor, and you ended up sleeping at a steep angle. I didn't care. I just wanted to get warm.

"We're planning on getting up at twelve-thirty," said Jen. "Are you going to be able to go that soon?"

I laughed in a dry whisper, "I'd better be. I guess if I can't make it then your boss certainly doesn't have to pay me."

"The point is we need to get there," said Rob.

"OK," I said, "I can get there."

Impossibly, I couldn't sleep. It was a lot colder down near the floor than on the upper bunks, and I was freezing. I knew I wasn't going to dry out very much in two hours. I kept shivering and I was hungry, but I didn't want to bang around cooking because my job was to be helpful customer service, not the annoying person who keeps waking everyone up in the middle of the night.

I was still awake when their alarm went off. It went off a long time, and nobody stuck a hand out to turn it off. I wondered if they had earplugs in. It didn't matter to me why they weren't getting up, their deep slumber was my salvation. The alarm finally shut itself off after fifteen minutes of beeping. I could hear the guide service down below, people yelling to one another in the dark, banging the outhouse door, getting ready to start their daily climb to the summit. I prayed the glaciologists wouldn't hear it.

"Shit!" I opened my eyes inside my communal sleeping bag and hit the light on my watch. It was four-thirty. "Wake up everybody, the alarm didn't go off!" Rob was grumbling. He was tinkering with it when I stuck my head out of the bag. "Everything looks like it's set right, but I didn't hear it at all. Did you hear anything?" he asked me, looking down.

"No," I said, getting up dizzily, "not a thing. It looks like it's going to be a beautiful day, though," I added, keeping it positive. I smiled in the pre-dawn light. I opened the door, and the sky to the east was a brilliant lightning pink.

Rob said, "The equipment we need you to carry is sitting on the storage box out front." I went out to look at it. There was a heavy metal pipe with about a five-inch diameter, maybe six feet long; a piece of thick PVC pipe, cut in half lengthwise that fit around the metal pipe; a metal crosspiece handle; and a bunch of one-inch aluminum pipes, also six feet long, secured together with a bungee cord. I strapped them on my pack like skis, with the big pipes on one side and the small ones all bunched together on the other side, and I used the bungee cord to tie both together about four feet above my head. There was also a Ziploc bag of miscellaneous tools, wrenches, screwdrivers, bolts, and screws, which I threw on top of my pack. It was awkward and top-heavy, and I had to sit down on the box and shrug into the shoulder straps while Rob held the contraption upright in order for me to put it on. When we started out I realized that the pipes banged into the back of my head, hard, with every step. It was a welcome distraction from my body's other aches and pains.

I'd filled my pockets with energy gel I'd been storing for an emergency. It was too expensive to use all the time, but now I was desperate for more energy. Trying one and then another, I decided

I liked the mixed berry—the chocolate tasted like dirt. I sucked them all down.

We stopped on the Ingraham Direct, about level with the top of the Cleaver, to take a snow core sample. It was going to be a warm day, the sky was azure blue above the clouds, and even the clouds below us had holes in them, revealing the green meadows and forest below.

Rob and Jen's project was to find out how fast the glaciers were melting. They were measuring snow density to determine the snow's water content, and they were also trying to find how deep last year's summer snow layer was. When we got to the first sampling location, on the side of the Cleaver, I noticed that the big metal pipe I had been carrying had teeth on it, and the handle attached to the top. Rob drove it down into the snow like a giant drill bit. When the top of the big pipe had been drilled in until it was level with the snow, one of the smaller aluminum pipes attached to the top of it with a couple bolts, and it was driven in, and so on. The goal was to get the big pipe that would gather the core sample all the way down to the bottom of the glacier. Then we'd pull the whole contraption up.

Once we finished pulling up the samples the snow we gathered from the bottom of the glacier would be slid gently into the half PVC pipe. Then Jen and Rob would look for layers, measure them, and determine their density, noting the depth and location of the core sample. My job was to write all the information down on a little pad of graph paper. On this first sample the pipes got stuck, frozen probably, deep in the hole, and I was glad for the reprieve while Rob swore and banged on the sides of the exposed pipe to try to free it.

As we continued up to the summit, my legs couldn't keep up the pace. They shook incessantly and would not acknowledge my directing them to go faster. I cursed at them. "Hey Rob," I said, "I need to slow down here for a bit. I'm so sorry. It's been kind of a long week." He didn't offer to take the equipment from me, so I figured we must have been going fast enough.

We headed into the summit crater to take another core sample. I had my down jacket on, but when the drill got stuck again and we had to dig it out, I had to take the jacket off because I got so warm shoveling. It felt good to be warm, but I was out of food now, and I was anxious to start heading down. We only had two shovels, and so we took turns, two of us digging and one taking a break and wearing the down jacket.

We got the drill out after an hour or so, but then Rob suggested that we dig down to the dirt so we could get a really good look at the different layers. The spot they picked was close enough to the edge of the crater that it seemed like a plausible thing to do, so we kept digging. Although there was softer snow on top, as we got deeper it got icy, and the layers were compacted together so tightly we had to alternate digging with a shovel and an ice ax. As we got deeper, the hole got smaller and eventually one person had to be down in the hole, handing up blocks of snow to another person kneeling on the edge and leaning over to get them. At some point during my break I fell asleep and Jen and Rob threw shovelfuls of snow on me, but I didn't wake up so they decided to let me stay there. I felt bad afterwards and told them I was on the clock and they should have woken me up. It turned out the snow was too deep for us to hit the ground, and we had to abandon the dig. I can't say I wasn't relieved.

Just as we finished shoveling snow back in the hole so nobody accidentally fell in it, a helicopter suddenly nosed up in front of us from the other side of the crater rim, and flew low over us. It was the rest of the climbing rangers, getting certified to use the jungle penetrator on rescues. The jungle penetrator is a little anchor-shaped thing on a winch attached to the belly of a Chinook helicopter that can lower you down and suck you back up while it hovers above you. This setup, a big helicopter with a winch, is good for inserting people into tight places or for high-altitude rescues where a smaller helicopter wouldn't have the power to land and then take off again.

It had been completely quiet while we were digging the hole in the summit crater, but now the wind from the rotors blew our stuff everywhere, while the rangers waved at us. We were glad when, after their initial buzz-by, they flew off to do their practice elsewhere. It had probably taken them less than ten minutes from the helibase below Longmire to get to the summit. It dawned on me that they'd known about this certification opportunity and, since someone had to go with the glaciologists, that's probably why I'd been asked.

We packed up and headed down to Camp Schurman, stopping for a couple more core samples. It was a beautiful day, but the carry-over and the sampling and the pit digging had taken forever, and it was almost five in the afternoon when we finally got to camp. Glenn had been dropped off at Schurman by the Chinook earlier in the day and he'd brought lots of homegrown vegetables from his garden. He offered to make dinner for us.

The social situation between me and Glenn was delicate, because we hadn't talked since that bad evaluation the previous year. I felt I needed to make good conversation to smooth things over, to let him know I wasn't upset and that I was trying to remedy my shortcomings by doing things like this very trip. But I was too tired to make any sort of decent conversation. I had a bad headache from spending so long in the sun without water and with the pipe banging a dent into the back of my skull. I decided what I really needed was a nap, even though I knew if I wasn't good I needed to at least be entertaining. I should be funny, I told myself, and then we could all have a good talk, Rob,

Jen, Glenn, and me. I could pull everything together. Everything would be fine again. I could help make dinner, get things ready for the next day's march down to White River. Except at that moment I couldn't do any of those things. I had to go to bed because I felt like I was dying.

The Schurman hut is a lot nicer than the Muir hut. It's about five times the size. When you come in the door there are benches running along both sides big enough to sleep on, and a bunk hanging from the ceiling on the left. Further back there are cabinets for food, a stereo system, a heater, a ladder, and then further back still there's a big kitchen with tons of storage room. Up the ladder is a windowed loft where extra people can sleep and where all the rescue gear, personal gear, and other, stranger things are stored. I crawled up the ladder and pulled out a communal sleeping bag. It had "ASS BAG" written in Sharpie pen on the top in big letters. I got into it fully clothed.

Glenn handed up my dinner on a plate. They have real plates at Schurman; they don't just eat out of the communal pot like we did at Muir. He'd made pasta and put some steamed broccoli rabe from his garden on the top. It was so sweet of him, and I was so tired I started to tear up. It was a tasty dinner, but the long, long stems on the broccoli rabe left me thinking I was chewing sticks. I would start in on one, but no matter how long I chewed it, it never seemed to get any smaller or mushier, and in the end I carefully ate around them and left them on the plate next to my bed. "Thanks Glenn, that was really tasty," I yelled down the ladder, wishing there was a way I could get more of the pasta without more of the odd vegetable.

A minute or two later Jen came up and I got up to help her make her bed next to mine. She pulled out a sleeping bag that had "HO BAG" written on it, and she looked at it and sighed. I started giggling, wondering exactly what went on in these bags and knowing that I really didn't want to know. She had to cover her mouth with her hand and I had tears running down my face. I had to sit down again, partly because I was laughing so hard and partly because the room was spinning. I offered to trade bags with her, but she said she thought the "ASS" bag might be worse. Down the ladder, Glenn and Rob were talking about the joys of gardening, Glenn's newfound passion, until they finally fell asleep.

We set the alarm for five-thirty, with the plan to leave by six so we could get down before the snow got too soft. In the morning I waited until I thought I heard Glenn step outside. "Is Glenn down there?" I yelled down the ladder. "No, he just went to the bathroom," said Rob from the kitchen. I grabbed my dinner plate with the broccoli rabe sticks and beelined it down the ladder and over to the garbage can, flipped open the lid with the neat foot pedal and shoveled the little sticks into the trash with my back to the front door. I looked up and Rob was staring at me with an amused expression on his face. I shrugged and smiled but he looked past me, and when I turned around there was Glenn in the doorway looking sad. "You didn't like the organic vegetables from my garden?" And there was nothing I could really say after that. As we were leaving, Glenn handed me the trash to take down. It looked like a week's worth or more.

The garbage wouldn't fit under the lid of my pack with the pipes on it, so I duct-taped the huge garbage bag to the gear loops on the back of my pack. I had to lean way forward to balance the pipes already, and the black bag accentuated the hunchback effect. The first five steps or so out of camp on the rocks were OK, but an ice crust had formed over the soft snow. It was thick enough that Rob and Jen could walk on the firm surface easily, but with the glaciologists' equipment and the garbage and the fact that I wasn't real tiny to begin with, the crust wouldn't hold me. With every step it would hold for a second when I first put my foot on it, then I would crash down through knee-high soft, unconsolidated snow and the pipes would come down after me and bean me on the head. It was slow and exhausting and I couldn't keep up. I was glad that we stopped after only a few hundred yards to take another snow sample so I could take a break.

All the time while Rob was dealing with the drill, I was trying to decide what to do. Things could not go on this way. The weight was too much. My head hurt terribly already. My legs were too weak. There comes a point when a person has to sacrifice her dignity, her professional credibility, her gear, and everything else to simply get home. Forget having a job next season; this was about personal survival.

I pulled one of my prusiks off the rope that tied us all together. We used the rope, with one of us tied into each end and one in the middle, in case any of us fell into a crevasse. The other two of us would then catch that person before they fell too far in, and then we'd pull him out. The prusiks, which were tied loops of five-millimeter cord, were dual-purpose: they could be used either to make a pulley system so we had more leverage to pull someone out, or the fallen person could use them to maneuver himself out of the crevasse. I had a spare prusik, so I took off my pack and looped the prusik around the pack's hip strap, clipping the other end to the back of my climbing harness. My pack was now trailing behind me. I figured the pipes would act like a rudder and with the garbage on the top, the whole thing wasn't likely to flip over. I knew it would slide on top of the icy crust, but I'd never seen anyone drag their pack before. Sleds yes, but not here, and packs, definitely no. It seemed like a horribly juvenile thing to do, very un-ranger-like. The looks that Rob and Jen were giving me confirmed my suspicions. "I've never done this before," I explained. "I just don't know what else to do."

It worked like a dream. Without my pack I was light enough that I stayed up on the crust. The pack tracked straight and true behind me. I could tell the pack was taking some damage around the edges from the ice, but it seemed like a small price to pay. Rob was worried that his expensive equipment would fall out of the pack and slide away down the hill, but I assured him it was strapped in tight, and it was.

Instead of going down the standard way, down the Inner Glacier, we planned to go down the Emmons to its terminus. Rob wanted core samples, and he had some permanent PVC snow stakes there that he wanted to take measurements on. We weren't sure we would be able to make it down since the glacier was fairly broken already, but he really wanted to go that way, and he was running this trip.

Finally, I could see the bottom of the glacier, and we were close to the trail that would take us back to the car. But the section of glacier we were on was very broken. It looked like an apple fritter, with the slots cut in the top, and my stomach rumbled at the thought. Then I squinted out at the snow that was as impossible to look at as the sun, and at the glacier's thousands and thousands of dark blue holes promising a quicker way out than hiking down, and what I saw didn't look anything like food, fritter or otherwise. It looked impassible.

Despite Rob's protests I said we couldn't continue this way. The glacier was too broken and we were going to fall in. I was right, but being right meant we had to hike back uphill to get off the glacier higher up. We turned around and started back. It was nice to know that, despite my struggles with the pack weight and my slow pace, I'd actually helped the expedition out.

On the three-mile trail back to the parking lot I tripped on a root and did a face plant in the dirt, breaking one of the trekking poles I'd borrowed from Adrienne (I'd already broken both of mine earlier in the week). Replacing it would mean I'd actually *lost* money by doing this trip. I had to rationalize quickly, because I wanted to cry. Most people climb the mountain for fun, not for money, I told myself. Mountains shouldn't be climbed for financial reasons; it's too much work for the money.

I'm not sure climbing mountains is fun, either. In fact, I'm sure it's not. The camaraderie that often comes from climbing, especially with friends, is absolutely worth it. The view may be worth it. The feeling of having your body running smoothly is wonderful—and being done with it, having done it, is nice. I was ready to be done with this climb.

We made it to the car at White River Campground, and two hours later I was dropped off at the Paradise dorm. We said our goodbyes. I said, "Thanks so much," and limped away to my car. It had a flat tire, and my spare was flat. One more impediment. I smiled. This one wasn't going to stop me. I borrowed a bicycle pump and set to work on the spare with a vigor I didn't know I still possessed. I hugged the curves down between Paradise and Longmire, and I flipped the park off on my way out of the entrance station. (Not the attendant, just the job.)

An hour and a half later I was in South Hill in line at Safeway, my hair a bird's nest, my clothes reeking and bloody from the header on the trail, my eyes bloodshot, my hands shaking. But I was holding a beautiful pint of Ben & Jerry's Phish Food. Moments later I was sitting outside on the curb, consuming it. And that part, the being done part, really was great.

5

JUST A PAINFUL WAYPOINT

THE REST OF MY DAYS OFF PASS IN A BLUR. I come back to a Rainier Mountaineering client hit by rockfall while climbing Fuhrer Finger. He has sustained an open tib/fib fracture. RMI has lowered him on a rope down the Finger to the Wilson Glacier and the park has flown me up to get him, then we have both been dropped off at Harborview Medical Center in Seattle, the regional trauma hospital.

After he's been admitted I sit in the ambulance bay, my old stomping grounds from my stint as an EMT in Seattle, waiting for a park volunteer to drive the three hours up to get me. Maybe it's that I am wearing an ancient military flight suit and holding a backpack with brutal-looking ice tools bristling out of it between my knees while the hospital security guards stare at me through the bay door, or maybe it's being grubby in the city surrounded by old friends wearing white, but I feel rusty and embarrassed. I've forgotten how to act in a city, I'm sitting on a street corner with the other homeless people, and I've forgotten my wallet so I've got no money to buy food, either.

Two days later I set out from Paradise in the middle of the night. It has already been a long day. I expected to spend the rest of my shift at Muir, but a climber got altitude sickness and I helped him down. Now I need to get back up. A helicopter is coming to Muir first thing in the morning, and before the contraption shows up I need to corral a pile of construction waste and other refuse in boxes, put the boxes into big plastic nets, tie up the nets, and then, when the helicopter arrives, thread the swivels on the nets onto a cable hanging off the bottom of the ship so that the lot can be flown off the mountain. The whole job will take less than an hour, but getting back up to Muir so I can do it is going to take forever.

I wait longer to leave than I should. I stay in Paradise to make a meal, macaroni and cheese again, and a glass of Gatorade made from the powder. Before heading out, I have to dry out my jacket, pants, green shirt, and socks and gloves. I peel them off my body and throw them in the dryer, plugging in quarters I borrowed from Adrienne's room.

I eat my dinner out of the pot, in the basement sitting in front of the dryer in my bra with my backpack across my lap to cover me in case anyone comes downstairs. When the cycle finishes I get dressed. My clothes are stiff and they smell like me, which is to say sweat, chili powder, and ranch salad dressing. It has been five days since I washed them, but there isn't time now.

I carry my heavy, wet boots upstairs with the laces biting into my hand. I duct-tape over the raw spots on my heels and the outside of my little toes, the holes in my skin that seem to get deeper and bloodier every time I pull the old tape off. My feet burn when I pull my boots on. The pain of the first few steps makes my eyes water.

I'm only going back up to Muir for one more night, and I don't want to bring anything up with me, since the weight would only make the trip harder. For one more night, I can live without a lot of things. I put a quart of water and a chocolate bar in my pack and swing it onto my back. It will be cold, I tell myself, but I won't stop. I'll be OK if I keep moving.

I remember that my backpack used to be red. Now it is pink from the sun, with salt lines on the straps, and I have rub marks on my pants and on my hips where the pack rests.

Looking out into the darkness, I see myself reflected in the glass panes in the front door. I notice that it has been a long time since I've washed my hair. It has gotten shorter; barely long enough now to put up, and I wonder if this is because it has become so tangled. It is lighter, too, with white streaks from the sun, where it used to be the color of cherry wood with a dark stain. I feel myself fading, like my pack is fading. I haven't looked at myself in a long time. Nose to nose with my reflection, I see lines in the corners of my eyes from squinting at the snow—that blinding retinal pain in the morning—and I can't read anything from my own expression.

I walk out into the darkness, and the door clicks quietly behind me, locking me out. There are tiny green eyes in the dark, bouncing in the light of my headlamp. I use a small LED light that lasts for two weeks on one set of batteries, because batteries are expensive, but I can't see much farther than my own feet. Although I can't see it, I can hear a grouse in the blueberry bushes, along with the constant reassuring clicks of my ski poles on the concrete of the parking lot as I head out.

I won't start being paid again until six in the morning, and so my thoughts, at least, are my own. I turn off my Park Service radio even though we are supposed to be on call at all times. Later I'd say, if they tried to find me, that the volume was accidentally turned down. It is so much easier to continue this way, where only my body needs to keep moving for the man. My body is its own thing, disconnected from me, from everything. I barely have control over it. I've realized that my body can go on walking forever as long as I don't make it go too fast.

I am a disgrace to my work, to all the climbing rangers, because I am tired. I live in a world where a new speed record was just established at four hours and fifty-nine minutes from the parking lot at Paradise to the summit and then back again. Car to car in less than five hours. I am lucky on these nights just to make it to Muir in that time. My mind is like a brick in my skull, it's so heavy. It keeps trying to pull my head down to the pavement. I don't know if it's heavy with shame or with exhaustion. My breathing is that of a dreamer, deep and consistent. Everything around me is dark. I walk up through the black meadow. On both sides of me is the rich, cold, herbaceous vegetation, elbow-deep damp flowers. I can almost see them exhaling oxygen I need to help me continue on. I see them move in a breeze and it makes me shudder.

This walk makes me think of nothing. There are no sudden insights, no ruminations on the past or expectations of the future, no daydreams to break the monotony. The future is unbearable and the past is gone, and now there is only this moving like a ghost though the night. I cannot feel my feet, I am floating.

It gets colder as I go higher. The dew turns into frost on the few subalpine firs, and they glitter in my blue light. When I turn my head away, the trees disappear. There is frost on the rocks and frost on the trail, and no footprints but my own. I turn around to look at my tracks, to feel I've made solid progress, that I'm doing OK. My head is still numb, but there is a pain in my chest like a longing. I'm not sure for what—a bed somewhere, maybe, or that magical ability to be fast and solid and sure. It's something I remember having, so long ago.

I stare down at the imprint of my boot tread in the frost, and then up at the sky, and wish on all the stars to give me fire, but then they go out. I feel betrayed until I realize a moment later that I've fallen asleep. I open my eyes and the stars are back, and I find myself sitting on a pile of water bars, logs that the trail maintenance crew has left. It's too cold to stay there, and I get up and keep walking.

My nose is cold. It drips but I can't feel it. I only watch as the occasional drop plummets out of sight. I get to Pebble Creek, and the little stream is covered with a layer of swirling ice, full of little holes, the edge of each one coated with a fat layer of frost. It looks just like salt on the edge of a margarita glass. A thousand margarita glasses. *It's a party and I'm the only one here.* I leave it.

Everything from here up is on the snow. I sink down through an ice crust, about an inch with each step. It's the sound of something newly formed, breaking. I can see the shape of the mountain ahead of me in the dark. It glows, the enormous white glaciers glued to the rocks. It lies flat in front of me, from my feet to the stars, all of it glittering, all of it connected to thousands of years of old snow below me in black, dirty, crusty layers. Altogether, the mountain is a big thing to be with, alone in the dark.

When I stop, my head is in a cloud of my own breath. I'm thirsty and I take my pack off to get my water bottle. I'm dizzy when I stand up, and my stomach is a hard knot, like a ball of ice. The key to success on these trips is not stopping too much. The water is as cold as it can be without being ice. It makes my teeth hurt and I start shivering uncontrollably, but I know I will feel better the next day for not getting dehydrated now. Who knows what will happen tomorrow. I shiver harder, my legs rigid. I pull my pack back up to my shoulder in one slow, static movement, and the sweat on my back has turned cold. I keep my eyes focused on my destination only three thousand feet above me that I can see as clear as anything, at the base of the Cathedral Rocks.

My hair is covered in frost from my breath. Each strand that has fallen down had its own insulating layer of rough crystals. I can see the crystals in my eyelashes and freezing in the air. I keep walking. It's not far, I tell myself. There are people up there asleep in their little yellow and orange tents, which sometimes glow like Japanese lanterns but are now black cold nylon on spindly aluminum legs engulfing the sleepers in the dark. Muir is no destination, just a painful waypoint for people who always want to be somewhere else.

One by one, my fingers start to freeze. First the skin directly under the holes in my gloves, where I've had frostbite before, wearing these same gloves; then in a better semblance of order, from smallest to largest, my little finger, and then the next and then the next become hard and numb, still grasping my ski poles. I don't think about it. There is nothing to do but continue.

The snow gets harder, I no longer sink into it. I can walk along the ice crust, which is slick sometimes and I have to be careful where I put my feet. It takes as much energy as I can muster to concentrate on the ground. I no longer look up or at my watch with its altimeter, because it doesn't matter anymore. There is no destination, there is only this. Only the sound of my breath and the mountain under me, and above me, and surrounding me.

I am too tired. I need to lie down. I take my pack off and pull out my chocolate bar for energy—I curl up on top of the pack in the fetal position and put my arm over my head, hiding from the mountain and the cold. I try to eat the chocolate bar, but it won't melt in my mouth so I chew it like gravel, and can't swallow it.

I know I can't sleep here. I've tried it so many nights before, because of whatever circumstances, wet in the snow in the middle of the night, lying down until the shivering became an exhausting rigidity, and my fingers and toes feel obligated to start moving. If I stayed I would lie here, cramped and afraid to lose the heat I've trapped by moving, and sometimes my mind would drift, but I'd never get to sleep. I get up again and it is terrible, the continuing, but it's also comforting because it is the same. It is a routine that I follow step after step and in this, for once, I always know what will happen next.

After an interminable distance, miles and miles and days and days without a sunrise, I come to my own door. The plywood

A-frame in the sky. The whole camp is quiet, but I can see high above me tiny lights on the Cleaver, other people climbing in the dark. I feel no kinship with them, they are distant and involved in a quest I no longer understand. I open the door, smelling mold and wet feathers, and I go inside where nobody and nothing can see me. It is a relief. I take off my boots, which don't hurt anymore, and I get into a doubled sleeping bag on the bunk in the back, one inside another, and lay down.

I am wet, the nylon of the bag sticks to my wet socks as I try to slide in. The bag is cold and I wonder if I have enough energy to produce heat, to warm the bag up and dry out. With wooden fingers I set the alarm for three hours' sleep, and I smile.

6

BACKTIED TO A BUSH

EARLY JULY WAS CHOCK-FULL OF RESCUES. In a little over a week, a Rainier Mountaineering Incorporated client was seriously injured when he was hit by icefall on the Kautz. Another RMI guide and three of his clients fell two hundred feet down the Ingraham glacier, sustaining femur fractures, serious head injuries, and spinal injuries, resulting in a very involved rescue and media firestorm. Then two north side rangers spent the night at 13,500 feet in subzero temperatures on the Emmons Glacier with two people injured in a fall and three hypothermic would-be rescuers. The winds were so strong that their tent collapsed; that one was later described to me as "a rough night."

When my shift started, I scrambled to keep up with the backlog of maintenance projects that had been put on hold, since rescues justifiably take precedence. By day seven of my shift I was happy to have a day working with Adrienne in the Climbing Information Center, answering the phone and issuing climbing permits. The CIC is in the middle storey of the Guide House, a newly remodeled, big, formal, and furnitureless building filled with echoes. We had moved in from a much smaller building, and we didn't have nearly enough stuff to make this new space friendly or inviting.

On the walls, surrounding an immense open area, were brand-new information displays about the dangers of dehydration, cold, storms, lightning, avalanches, and inadequate mental preparedness, illustrated with pictures we'd taken of each other suffering. It was strange to see people I knew on display, since the building seemed so impersonal. There were also a lot of Mike's pictures of sunsets and sunrises, and a memorial display for two climbing rangers who'd died a few years ago, doing a rescue in a storm. Maybe we were insensitive, but Adrienne and I took it down and moved it to the back office, facing the wall. We didn't want to see their faces looking at us while we worked. I know it gave me the creeps.

A new video featured Andy and Glenn demonstrating an easy step-by-step process for using a "blue bag" in the wilderness. First, take the blue plastic bag and use it as a glove to pick up your own shit and toilet paper. Get one finger under the edge with your other hand and invert the blue bag, and use one of the provided twist ties to secure the top. Then place the blue bag into the clear plastic bag, also provided, and use the remaining twist tie to secure the outer bag. Put the packaged waste in an outside pocket of your pack and continue on with your climb, happy with the knowledge that the drinking water will be cleaner and the route more beautiful because you've picked up your own crap. This was important. Every time we found human waste someone left on the mountain, we had to pick it up. We typically picked up several finds a day while we were climbing.

Kids liked the video. They ran around in circles listening to the squeak of the newly refurbished wood floor under their feet, and every time the video ended they ran over and pushed the button again. During the busiest weeks of the summer, enough kids and other tourists came through to keep the video playing in a continual loop. We could all recite it from memory. I didn't mind.

It was just nice to be inside today, sitting and resting and watching the video and the kids, and answering phone calls.

Adrienne was in the back doing paperwork. She was in charge of the CIC this year because she'd hurt her knee over the winter working as a ski instructor. She'd been holding the arms of a tiny girl who was skiing between her legs when the girl slipped sideways and their skis tangled. Adrienne had had to ski the rest of the way down to the lodge on one leg while carrying the crying girl. Adrienne had had surgery on the knee in the spring and it was pretty much fine now, but she didn't want to risk hurting it again before it fully healed. I was kind of jealous. It seemed like it would be such a relief not to have to be hard, fast, and ready every day. Adrienne could decide each day whether or not it was a good day for her to go out and climb the mountain.

A couple of climbers were milling around, looking at the warning posters, waiting to register. They looked typical of the average younger-generation climbers who came to the park. Little knit hats on (despite the heat). Expensive sunglasses. Well-tanned and muscled, and wearing trendy approach shoes. They were discussing their plans and their past exploits loud enough that I could hear everything they said; they kept glancing at me to see if I was impressed. They were climbing Disappointment Cleaver, the most popular and perhaps easiest route on the mountain.

I ran their credit cards, handed over their passes and blue bags, and showed them a copy of the weather forecast. "I don't suppose there's anybody here who's climbed the mountain lately?" the one with the blue knit hat asked me, looking past me into the back room.

I noticed his eyes didn't linger on Adrienne either, hunched over at the computer with her blond braids hanging down her back. "Hey, Gator isn't here, is he, or is he out on the mountain right now?" Blue Hat sounded excited.

I continued to look at them, expressionless, but inwardly irritated. "Well," I said, trying to sound genuinely apologetic, mentally donning my customer service hat, "I climbed the DC yesterday, and I know the route pretty well. Our volunteer Tom might have climbed it this morning. I can give him a call on the radio if you'd like to hear the absolute most current conditions from him, or I can just give you yesterday's info." I meant this as a slight jab, since the weather had been consistent and we all knew nothing had changed at all on the mountain since yesterday. But I figured they'd see it as a chance to talk to a guy, without having to ask. Then I added, "And Mike is down in Longmire if you want to stop by and say hi."

"Oh," said Blue Hat, "We don't actually know him personally, just wondered if he was going to be out on the mountain at the same time as us."

"Sorry, no luck today," I said, smiling, and then they asked me to give Tom a call.

It was ten to three. We closed at three. All the climbers planning on climbing today were long gone, and Adrienne and I were only waiting to close, hoping that no more tourists would come in and want to watch the blue bag video. It was hot outside but it was cold in this huge old building, and I couldn't wait to get out in the sun and soak it up, feeling it radiate into me.

The phone rang. Somebody had figured out how to make the ringer play *The Simpsons'* theme song. Most of the climbers who came in liked it, but it got annoying after the millionth time. Donny at the communications center was calling to ask me to check on an injured visitor hiking in the meadows.

"Hey Adrienne," I yelled into the back room, "Donny says there's a kid with a broken arm at Glacier Vista. Do you want to just close down the Center now and go with me up there? I mean, I think we can justify it because it's sort of heavy carrying the first-aid kit and the O_2 kit by myself, and it looks way more professional if there are two of us."

"Sounds good to me, anything to get me out of here," she said, with the front door keys already in her hand.

My feet were killing me as we headed out of the CIC. My constantly wet boots and the persistent cold had slowly destroyed my feet. I wasn't sure if I had trench foot or what, but large chunks were falling off the bottoms, and they were really painful. The whole mess had gotten worse earlier that week with huge blisters that had been rubbed off in a series of climbs, and now my heels were large, bleeding sores. I'd covered them with antibiotic ointment and duct-taped gauze over them.

That morning I'd tried to fit my feet into my Park Service-issue boots that go with my green ranger uniform, but they hurt too much. I could stand up after a minute or two, but I couldn't walk without an unprofessional limp. So I wore flip flops instead, in violation of the strict uniform policy. Now that I was headed outside I had to make sure no other rangers saw my feet. Backcountry, frontcountry, and law enforcement rangers already thought that climbing rangers got too many perks, like good raincoats and a synthetic uniform we could wear above ten thousand feet in bad weather. It was true. The rest of the park had to buy their own uniform raincoats, and they were lousy.

The trail was thick with visitors. They were everywhere, slowing us down, stopping right in front of us, cutting us off. We wove around them, saying, "Excuse us." "May we just squeeze by you." "You want to go left here to go to the overlook." "It's a green false-hellebore." "It doesn't sound like a bear, it was probably just a marmot."

At first the sun felt good. It was the height of summer in Paradise, and we were surrounded by amazing vistas: the Tatoosh across the valley, Goat Rocks, Adams, Hood, and Jefferson in the distance, tiny rivulets of water burbling out of dark grottoes surrounded by wildflowers at our feet. All of it being photographed by thousands of tourists surrounded by thousands of mosquitoes. We started sweating almost immediately, and after a few minutes the itchy green pants became a menace and our grey uniform shirts stuck to our backs. We'd both been spoken to about how unprofessional it was to undo the top button of our shirts just because it was hot, but I really wanted to anyway, and it took a lot of willpower not to mess with it. It's funny how the little things can become the most annoying.

We got to the intersection that leads to the top of Glacier Vista. "Is there a kid with a broken arm up there?" we asked a group of middle-aged women hiking down the trail.

"No, there's nobody up there like that at all. The view isn't even as good as they said it was in the ranger station."

"I'm sorry you didn't like the hike, but are you sure there aren't any kids up there?" Adrienne asked again.

"Yeah, we're sure." They kept walking past us and then looked back. "Hey, do you think the view is better from Pan Point or is it not worth the bother of hiking all the way up there, either?"

"Maybe it was a prank," said Adrienne. "I wonder how Donny found out, anyways." Cell phones don't work in Paradise, so somebody had to have walked out and reported the accident to a ranger in person. Trying to decide what to do, we looked around blankly at the myriad of people on various trails and walking through the flowers, despite the signs everywhere saying to stay on the trails. A woman in her early fifties, with closely cropped white hair, was walking fast and passing people on the stairs, coming down towards us. She started waving. "Are you rangers?" she asked us. I glanced briefly down at my uniform. "Yes."

"This kid," said the woman, waving behind her at a very overweight child who looked like he was about ten, wearing a red basketball jersey and black basketball shoes, "is the brother of the kid who hurt himself. This kid found me on the trail, and it was my friend Nancy who walked out to report the accident. I assume that's why you're here?" She trailed off and looked at us expectantly.

"Where is the injured kid?" I asked.

"Oh, I don't know," she said, agitated. "This little guy didn't know the names of any of the trails, so we couldn't tell where he'd come from. He's got a walkie-talkie, though." The sweaty boy held it up for us to see. "And his mom answers back sometimes. She's with the other one, the hurt kid."

"Thanks for your help," said Adrienne, turning to the boy. "Hey kid, do you think you could walk with us back to where your mom and your brother are?"

"Maybe." Adrienne and I looked at each other and I shrugged.

It was really hot here in the meadows and we hadn't thought to bring any water, since this wasn't supposed to take very long. I was already thirsty. And I was becoming confirmed in my suspicions that walking in flip flops up steep pavement with sweaty feet and a heavy first-aid kit sucked.

All my complaints started welling together and I wanted to sit down in the shade—just sit for a while with my eyes closed. I wanted all the tourists to disappear with their noise and problems and questions, and I wanted to lie in the meadow, where nobody was allowed to go, and look up at the pale blue sky, with my entire peripheral vision filled with cold purple lupine.

The kid lagged behind us, wheezing and tripping along. He was spent. I let him go on in pain a minute or two longer than I should have, but I was irrationally angry with him for having a brother who had hurt himself and had interrupted my afternoon napping plans. We came to a trail intersection, where three different trails came together, and I asked him if he knew which way he'd come from. He looked around without comprehension. His eyes were glazed over from the heat and the strain and thirst, and he obviously had no idea where he was.

There was still a steady stream of people hiking past us, back down to Paradise. I stopped an older couple wearing matching khaki sun hats. "Hi, I'm Bree, and this is Adrienne. We're the rangers up here today, but we're dealing with an incident in the meadows. This boy really needs to get down to Paradise, and we're concerned he might not make it down there by himself. Would you guys mind if he tagged along with you?" They were nurturers, we'd chosen well. They asked him if he wanted any water. I looked at the water bottle as they handed it over, and I watched him drink, spilling half the contents on his shirt. I couldn't take my eyes off it. "Just drop him off at the Paradise Inn," I said. "We'll make sure there's somebody's there to get him. And thanks so much."

I called it in on the Park Service radio. "Comm. Center, 686."

"Comm. Center."

"We still haven't found the injured visitor, but we did find his brother and he's hiking down to the Paradise Inn with some other visitors. Could you alert the Inn to keep him there until we can come get him?"

"We'll call the Inn, let us know when you find the injured party," said Donny.

"Well, Adrienne, shall we try the walkie-talkie?" I asked. Adrienne pushed the button on the front of the little blue unit. "This is Adrienne from the Park Service. Can the person that needed help hear me?" We waited a second and then there was the sound of a woman screaming hysterically on the other end. This was discouraging.

"Ma'am, can you tell us where you are?" Adrienne spoke slowly and clearly into the piece of blue plastic. Some of the people walking by stopped to listen while pretending to take pictures or gaze out into the meadow. There was more screaming and crying. It seemed like this mother was overreacting to a broken arm, but then, I supposed she had been waiting a while for help.

"Ask her if she can hike out with the kid back to Paradise," I said. "Can both of you hike back down to Paradise?" Adrienne said into the walkie-talkie.

"Both of us?" the woman said, sounding confused. "Noooo." And the "no" turned back into a wail, then back into sobbing.

"Do you know where you are?"

There was a pause.

"Mount Rainier?" came the hesitant answer.

"Oh dear," I said. "Maybe we should just keep hiking uphill and see if we can see them, because they obviously aren't here."

We kept going higher. They could have been anywhere on the miles of trails that wind back and forth, crisscrossing each other. Adrienne kept asking questions. "Are you on a trail?" "Are you on snow?" "Are you in the trees?" "Can you see Paradise?" "Are there other people with you?" The woman didn't know very much, and we had a hard time understanding anything she said because she was screaming into the little walkie-talkie speaker.

"I think she's off the trail," said Adrienne finally. "Great," I said. Every couple of minutes we asked the people coming the other way if they'd seen an injured kid, but nobody had. We hiked up to Alta Vista and wondered briefly if the mom and her son could be over the side towards the Nisqually Glacier, but peering down through the trees from the trail, we didn't see anybody. Uphill was Panorama Point.

"Did you go uphill to Panorama Point?" Adrienne asked the walkie-talkie. There was no reply.

"Maybe we're out of range?" I wondered.

Adrienne wiped her face with her sleeve and didn't answer.

Ed Dunlevy, the head law enforcement ranger and EMS coordinator, called us on the radio asking if we needed any help. "Well," I said, "I'm not sure, since we haven't found the injured boy yet. If we don't find him soon, we could use a few more people to help look for him."

"OK" said Ed. "I'll be incident commander on this, so I'll be in Paradise and you can talk to me directly when you call in."

I thought it must be a slow day in Paradise for us to get so much attention. I wondered why sometimes I couldn't get help when my life depended on it, and other times the whole park was willing to come out. To some extent it depended on which budget the money was coming out of. If the total cost for the call was less than five hundred dollars, then it came out of the climbing budget, which meant we needed to keep it as cheap as possible. No extra people, no overtime—when the climbing budget was expended, we got laid off. If the total cost was over five hundred dollars, then the money came out of the park's search and rescue budget, which had much deeper pockets. I figured that Ed was betting it would take more than me and Adrienne to splint a broken arm, it would take enough people to go over the five hundred dollar mark. While I was happy for the help, I was also a little pissed that he didn't think we could do this by ourselves.

Tom called me, saying that he was headed down from Camp Muir, could he help? If there was a rescue and the money was flowing, he could get paid for his time, even though he was a volunteer. I thought it would be good for him financially, and good for knocking the total cost up into the search and rescue budget. "Sure, Tom. And could you bring an extra quart or two of water down with you? We'll meet you at Pebble Creek." The water request was unusual, since it takes hours of melting snow to get even a little water at Muir, but I was getting desperately thirsty. I looked

over at Adrienne, who seemed pleased that she was out of the CIC
for a while, and I envied her enthusiasm and vigor.

Pebble Creek is just uphill from Panorama Point, about two-
fifths of the way to Camp Muir. The snow ends there in a series of
dirty, icy rolls leading down to the small creek. Nobody up here
had seen an injured kid, either. We both doubted that the group we
were looking for would be any higher than this. Most people turn
around at Pebble Creek, if they get that far, unless they specifically
want to climb up to Muir. Tom said he'd keep an eye out on his way
down, just in case.

We'd been hiking for an hour and I wanted a break. We had
to wait here for Tom, anyway. Adrienne checked out some of the
little snow pockets between the rocks that we couldn't see from
where we were, in case it was possible for a person to get stuck
in one. We were high enough that nothing but heather and a few
penstemons and asters grew in little clumps between the rocks. I
sat down on a rock next to a patch.

There were a few day trippers coming down from Muir, and
I said hi to everybody as they passed me. "Taking a break, huh?"
said one guy with a large orange backpack. I smiled. "I wish I had
your job, sitting in the sunshine, looking at the mountains all day. I
only get to do this on vacation. Hey, what do you have to do to be
a ranger anyway? My son is in high school and he's getting a little
chunky, if you know what I mean." The man threw me a conspira-
torial smile, which I took to mean the kid was huge. "And he needs
a summer job, where do I sign him up at?"

"Well," I said, "the median age for a climbing ranger is over
thirty, and I think you're supposed to have a degree in something,
you know, nature-related. It's also best to be in shape before you
start, and it's good to know something about climbing early on.
There's always a chance, though, right?" I was trying to keep the
conversation light, but my voice started to have an edge. "Hey,

what do you do? My knees are starting to go and I'd like to have a job where I can get out of the weather once in a while." Things went on like this as I tried to hold it together.

Finally, Tom showed up, and I waved at Adrienne to come back the next time I saw her head pop up from behind a boulder pile. We'd come up here on one side of the Skyline Trail, and we decided that we should try going down the other side, checking out the various trails as they branched off on our way back down. I felt much more enthusiastic after chugging the quart of water Tom had brought. "You're an angel," I told him, "bless you." Glenn called on the radio and said he was taking over as Incident Commander. Ed and the Cougar Rock Campground Host were going to check out the trails just outside of Paradise to see if they could find the kid down there.

Adrienne had been trying the walkie-talkie periodically, and as we dropped down from Pan Point on the other half of the Skyline Trail loop we picked up the hysterical mother again. "Where are you guys?" the woman wailed.

"Where are you?" Adrienne replied. "Do you know where the nearest trail is? Could you start walking down it to the nearest trail intersection and read the signs so you can tell us where you are? That would help us out a lot."

"OK, I'll send the kids," said the woman.

"What kids?" Adrienne wanted to know, and then as an afterthought she added, "Hey, are there any landmarks around you that we might be able to recognize?"

"No," the mother cried, "there's nothing here but the damn waterfall."

I called Glenn to let him know. "IC, 686."

"Go ahead, Bree." I felt important with my name going out over the radio after having used a number for so long.

"I guess they're near a waterfall. Could you look at the map and give us a list of all the waterfalls next to trails around here?" I knew there were a bunch. Glenn said he'd look when he had a minute.

The three of us were half-jogging down the dusty trail in the late afternoon sun. There weren't as many trees and bushes on this side. It was mostly just shale and a few disconnected snow patches, but that also meant better visibility—we could see a long ways down. There didn't seem to be anyone out on the trails at all. This side of the Skyline isn't nearly as popular. Most people go up and down the same way since doing the whole loop takes longer. It was also getting late, and I was sure that anybody in their right mind would have headed back to Paradise for dinner at this point.

Although the trail is one of the most rigorously maintained in the whole park, a lot of it is gravel and stairs. The section we were on consisted of large uneven stone steps, and it was really hard on the knees. I noticed that all three of us were limping slightly as we descended. Tom was carrying a big black plastic bag of garbage, smashed under the lid on his pack and ripe in the sun. He was ahead of me on the trail—I could see Paradise below us, and then it would be obscured behind the garbage, and then reappear again every time he took a step.

We were getting lower. It was a pity to have gained so much altitude just to lose it again. After a bit, we were totally out of the snow and back into alpine meadow with short little trees that came to our shoulders. I noticed that the flowers on this side were in better shape than on the west half of the trail, and I made a mental note to start recommending this side to hikers again. Glenn called us back on the radio and said there were a lot of waterfalls in the area. He sounded grumpy, and we wondered why he was in the park at all since these were his days off.

We came to the intersection of the Skyline with the Golden Gate Trail. There was a waterfall here, and we left the main trail and headed through the meadow on a social trail, made by visitors tromping on the vegetation until it died, to get a better look at it. There wasn't a lot of water coming down, since most of the snow patches that fed it had already melted. The waterfall was probably a hundred feet from top to bottom, but it wasn't vertical, it just ran down in a series of steeper steps, and in between them the water fanned in a thousand tiny, frothy fingers around the moss on the slimy black rock. About halfway up we could see people, not in the falls but right next to it sitting in the grass and hellebore and blueberry bushes. They waved, and we headed up the slope towards them.

It was steep and the grass was wet with mist from the falls. We had come in from the side, not the bottom, so if we slipped from where we were, we would keep going all the way to where the last cascade ended in a pile of jagged rocks another fifty feet below us. I grabbed handfuls of flowers, trying to hold onto enough of them that the roots would stay in the ground and hold me. My flip-flops didn't exactly have tread on them, and they kept sliding. I would start to slip and would press my whole body against the side of the slope, hoping the friction would be enough to stop me.

My mind wasn't into this. I had liked being on the trail, solidly connected to the earth. I didn't want to have to worry about falling to my death today. I just wanted to splint this arm and then go eat dinner like all the other hikers. I looked up and I could see that Adrienne and Tom had reached the accident site. They were on the other side of a small tree that was sticking out of the slope at an odd angle, like it too was slowly sliding off the cliff. I willed myself to continue crawling up the slope.

I wondered where my guts had gone over my seasons as a climbing ranger. I was supposed to be heroic. I'd been hired to rescue people willy-nilly, and yet here I was, proving I was the kind of person who had to think twice about risking my skin to save an injured child. A few weeks before, one of the north side rangers told me that the major reason I wasn't picked to do big rescues was that he thought I would someday be under a huge ice fall, running with seracs crashing all around me, and I would freeze up and get squished. He said you always had to be ready to die. Willing even. Excited maybe. But no matter what, you just had to go for it. I decided that my problem wasn't that I froze up, scared witless in the heat of the moment, I was OK once I had committed. My problem was far worse: before I would commit, I had to calculate my willingness to rescue an injured child versus the likelihood that I would die.

When I reached the tree I clutched at it, then straddled it, took my flip-flops off, and threaded them through my belt. It was better barefoot. I could dig my toes into the dry flakey dirt and use them to grasp at the tiny green plants.

When I finally made it over to everybody else, I asked Adrienne, "Did you do introductions?" trying not to show how badly I was shaking.

"Not yet," she said.

"Well, I'm Bree, and this is Tom and Adrienne, and we're the rangers up here on duty today."

I paused. "What's going on?" I whispered to Adrienne.

"The boy fell over the top of the waterfall, landed on his face, bounced down lower, then landed on his knees in the water over there. Somehow he managed to stop himself. His mom, his sister, and two brothers crawled up here and then his mom drug him out of the water and put him over here where it was a little flatter."

I looked around. The boy was covered with blood. He looked about twelve. He was half-sitting, half-lying on the steep grass. He had one butt cheek on a flat rock, but he had to hold onto the grass and brace with his foot to keep from sliding down over the next steeper section. The mother was standing, braced against a dead log that looked like it had a dubious connection to the earth. There was nobody else there.

"Where are the two brothers and the sister?" I asked.

"I guess we met one brother at Glacier Vista, and the two others, ages four and six, were sent back to the trail by their mother to alert us to their location here," said Adrienne. "And since we never met them, I'm assuming nobody knows where they are right now."

I got out my radio. "IC, 686."

"Go ahead, 686."

"We've located the injured party above the Golden Gate Trail. Uh. The injured party fell over the waterfall here, and due to the location we're either going to need a helicopter to winch him out, or we're going to need a rigging crew to do a lower down the waterfall, along with all the gear to do the lower. We also need an advance party, maybe Charlie if he's around, to run up the trail with some pickets and a light rope and a harness to secure the patient and rescuers to the slope."

"Great," growled Glenn over the radio. He sounded pissed. "It's too late to get a military helicopter today. I'll see what we can do about getting the people together to do a lower."

"Oh, also, Glenn, the mother here has two young children, ages four and six, who are on their own on the trails, so if everybody could keep an eye out for them it would be great."

I put the radio back in my pocket and crawled slowly over to where the kid was. "Hey, Adrienne, if you take the first-aid kit and stuff, could you brace yourself against that tree and then throw things to me when I ask for them?"

I turned to the boy. "Hi, I'm Bree, I'm one of the rangers up here. How's it going?"

He tried to say something, but his jaw was broken and there was a big chunk of skin that had come off his chin—when he tried to talk it rubbed against his chest and started bleeding again.

"Aw, it's OK, never mind," I said. "Hey, Adrienne," I yelled over, "how 'bout some roller gauze?"

I couldn't really tell what was wrong with him. He was wearing a Metallica sweatshirt, and his mom kept screaming that I wasn't allowed to cut it off. He'd just bought it with his own money and neither one of them could afford to get him a new one.

She got hysterical again when Adrienne threw me the scissors. "Just one sleeve," I said, eyeing the arm he was cradling in his lap. I cut the underside of the fabric up to above his elbow, despite her protests, and his forearm was angulated and fat and blue. His fingers were purple, but he could move them and I figured that was a good thing.

"Hey, Adrienne, throw me a SAM splint and some more roller gauze." I kept working. I wanted to take his blood pressure but I wasn't sure that I'd be able to get on his other side because it got steeper over there. I didn't want to crawl over him in case we bumped each other. The whole situation was so precarious that we'd probably both slide off.

I cut up his pants on the inside seams because his mother thought she'd be able to repair them later. He was still using one leg to brace himself. He had skinny, young, white legs. They were bruised and bleeding but looked mostly intact. He'd sprained or broken an ankle. I did a few more things, and got out the oxygen and squatted there with the bottle between my knees and one hand on a heather bush with thick roots.

Tom grabbed the radio out of my pocket; I told him to start arranging things for the people who were going to show up. Adrienne and Tom said they were going to try to take the mother up to the trail by way of the top of the falls. They said it looked easier to go up than down from where we were, and while they were up there they were going to start scouting for decent anchors. I yelled, "Good luck!" They started inching their way up the slope and some loose grass and dirt came down after they'd gone.

Then it was just me and the kid beside the waterfall. I missed them already. I started in on my inane cheerful chatter talk that I use with people who cannot talk back—a skill I just recently discovered I share only with dental hygienists and preachers.

Nothing happened for a long time. I watched the sun swing lower, behind the top of the gully. When we'd first arrived here the cool mist from the falls had been refreshing. But now the temperature was dropping and I embraced every last second in the sun. The shade line rushed at us and I realized it was going to be really cold in a few seconds. Because I couldn't move any further over to follow the sun, I held one arm out to touch it as long as possible, watching the darkness crawl down my arm to my fingertips.

The kid started shivering almost immediately, but I didn't have anything to put over him. I didn't even have a jacket. The oxygen bottle I was holding made my hands numb and I kept wiggling my toes to keep them from freezing in the wet grass. I kept talking for a while, but I eventually ran out of things to say. I could see a little bit of the trail below us, and I kept my eyes focused on it, watching for more rescuers. The kid started weeping, and I patted his shoulder. Later, when he couldn't hold onto the heather bush anymore, I got behind him and put my arms under his armpits and held him across the chest. He would still slide down in little slips, but every once in a while I would count to three and then heave him back uphill. He drooled blood on my hands.

I didn't see Charlie come up the trail, I only noticed him when he started crawling down the slope towards me covered in sweat with his jacket tied around his waist. He brought a harness and a short bit of rope. We put the harness on the kid and tied him to one of the tiny trees. I didn't trust the tree and we couldn't get the rope tight enough with the stretch, so it was more just in case he slipped and I couldn't grab him.

"Hey, Charlie," I said, "do you want your jacket or can I have it?" He handed it to me. "I could also really use a radio, and a sleeping bag for the kid, it's pretty cold down here." Charlie nodded and headed back up. I thought he was going to come back with more stuff, but he didn't.

It was dusk when I finally saw the crew headed up the trail below the falls. All of them in a line, with an old heavy litter they'd put a wheel on and filled with ropes and old rigging equipment. Andy had put together new lighter rigging kits, but they were locked up because they were valuable and only the supervisors had access to them. We'd never used them because it was always one of us who had to get the kits, and we weren't allowed to have the keys. I felt a flash of anger, but at the same time accepted that seasonal workers have always been considered untrustworthy, and climbing rangers doubly so since so much of the gear we needed for work was so easy to borrow for personal climbs and equally easy to forget to give back. There was no good solution. I made a conscious effort to be happy and think about getting rescued fast.

"Hey, look!" I said to the kid, "Here they are! I'm sure it won't be long now."

It took another interminable stretch of time until Charlie and a law enforcement ranger, Tim, carried the litter down the hill. They were awkwardly trying to crawl down, clutching the wire basket between them and hanging on to the verge with their outside hands. The litter was attached to slack ropes that ran back up the slope. I was a little disturbed by this because usually the whole bit, the people and litter, are lowered down on a tight rope from the top. When they got close I asked them what was up with the weird setup and Charlie said he didn't trust the anchors to take the full weight of himself, Tim, and the kid. So they weren't going to tie in, they'd just tie the kid in and then help push him back up the slope, hanging on to the rocks at the same time and hoping the anchors held if they accidentally dropped the litter.

"Oh," I said, nodding, thinking this was insanely risky. "Make sure the rope stays tight so it doesn't shock load your anchors if you do drop him."

I saw Tim eyeing me. He favored a militaristic, rule-based, cookie-cutter approach to all problems, which irritated me every time we met. Occasionally I would refuse to do what Tim wanted, which irritated him every time we met. As far as I was concerned, Charlie had gotten there before Tim, which meant that he was in charge, even though I'm sure Tim had some kind of incident management training that probably made him more qualified.

"Why are you down here without a helmet and a harness?" Tim said, pleased to have found something wrong with me. "That's very unprofessional, and it shows you didn't spend enough time thinking about safety awareness."

These lowland rescues are so different from rescues on the upper mountain. There's a certain flow on the mountain, everything is impromptu and nobody has all the right equipment, and we just do whatever works well. When the rest of the park is involved, the actual rescue often gets overlooked because everybody's worried about whether incident command, radio, and uniform protocols are being followed. I wondered if Tim realized how dangerous what he'd just done was. It's true he had a harness, but he wasn't tied to anything, and his helmet wouldn't be enough to save him if he slipped. "Sorry, Tim, I didn't realize I'd need a harness when I left Paradise."

"You always need to be prepared, Bree." I hate being spoken to in that tone of voice, part condescending, part motherly. I wondered what exactly I always needed to be prepared for. Tim continued to look me over, and when he got to my bare feet, only partially hidden in the grass, his eyes got wide. I knew he was going to have words with my supervisor's supervisor, the infamous Gator, and I was going to get some serious shit. I glared back and he slowly shook his head. Mike would understand my sore foot problem, but I also knew he wouldn't risk upsetting a law enforcement ranger by sticking up for me over a uniform issue. Uniform issues were really important, and my feet really weren't.

They'd brought a sleeping bag and they also had a backboard and a C-collar for the kid. I put the C-collar on him, trying to maneuver it around the broken jaw, but I didn't want to use the backboard. I knew he needed one, but there wasn't a good way to put him onto the board. If we put it down on the slope next to him, and he slid onto it, then he'd take off on it like a toboggan. Then, too, the litter had a weird slippery fabric lining, like the top of a trampoline, and I knew the backboard, with the kid on it, would slide out of the litter if it tipped at all, which of course it would. There was only one set of straps and there wasn't any extra webbing, so we could strap the kid down to the board or to the litter, but not both. I wanted to just tie him into the litter, get him to the top, and then deal with the backboard there.

Tim said no, there was a medical protocol to follow. I had a mental picture of the kid on the backboard, wearing his harness tied in to the rope with six feet or so of slack in it, sliding out of the side of the litter and being wrenched in the middle, probably knocking Tim and Charlie off, and maybe the shock load on the static ropes would be enough to make the whole system fail. Tim was demanding compliance and I kept looking at Charlie, but he didn't want to get in the middle of the argument.

I figured Tim was already pissed, what did it matter what I did at this point? I grabbed the backboard and dangled it behind me, over the water, where if I let go it would sail gently down to land in the pool fifty feet below. "I can drop it, Tim, or I can carry it up with me later." I stood there holding the red plastic backboard in one hand and clutching a Sitka valerian with the other, trying to look unfazed as my legs went numb and all the blood in my body rushed to my cheeks.

"Fine, I'll be in touch with your supervisor," said Tim. They called for tension on the ropes and then tied the kid onto the main line and slid him into the litter. The whole thing sagged down a couple feet and was ungainly enough without getting the backboard involved.

I inched back over to the tree where the first-aid kit was propped between a few branches, and started stuffing things back into it. I had to write up a run sheet for the ambulance people. I didn't want to look up and see how the raise was going. A lot of rocks and dirt came down and hit me. I hoped it was going fine. In the end, it did.

We cleaned up all the webbing from the scrawny trees and the bushes they were backtied to, and picked up the rigging kits. I carried the first-aid kit back down the hill in the dark. A medic had started hiking up after driving to the park from Tacoma, and she met us about halfway down the trail. Glenn had come into the field at some point to take over command of the rescue, and he ran ahead to talk to her about the kid's condition. I hadn't talked to Glenn, so I'm not sure how accurate the information exchange was. I asked him a bit later if I should give her a short report, but he said he'd handled it.

We wheeled the kid down in the litter from switchback to switchback in the dark. The trail was skinnier than two people abreast with the litter between them, and the grass was wet with dew, so the people on the outside slipped sometimes and we had to stop a lot so they could pick themselves up. I liked to look back and see everybody, a long line of headlamps bouncing in the dark—it was pretty, and there was a nice sense of togetherness. All the rangers out for a hike in the meadows on a moonless summer night. I would have liked to carry the litter all the way back to the Paradise parking lot, to make the feeling last longer, but someone had driven a truck on the lower trail so we put the litter in the back. I sat on the tailgate with the medic and gave her a short report anyhow, and then rode the rest of the way back to the parking lot. The kid groaned every time we hit a pothole.

The mom met us in the parking lot. Somebody had found her two youngest children on a trail and had dropped them off at the visitor center, and someone had gotten her other son from the Inn. Everybody was back together again. They were going to drive behind the ambulance to the hospital in Tacoma.

Tom, Adrienne, Charlie, Glenn, and I carried all the gear into the Paradise dorm, spread it out on the floor, and sorted it. We counted everything, daisy-chained all the webbing, put the equipment in duffle bags, and zip-tied them so none of us could steal anything. It was going to be dawn soon. I was excited, it was the last day of my eight-day shift.

When we were done putting away the gear I went upstairs and took a shower, feeling the hot water burn into all the cuts and scrapes I always seem to get on these crawling-through-the-brush days, even though I don't ever remember having hurt myself. Adrienne and Charlie went to bed. We all had to get up soon. I went into the dorm kitchen, turned all the lights on, and put some water on for mac and cheese, and while it was heating I lay down on the big, empty kitchen table. It was quiet and warm, just me and the moths fluttering around the ceiling lights. And I closed my eyes, just for a few minutes.

7

KAUTZ, SOLO

IT WAS SNOWING AND I WAS CRYING, HARD. It was newly dark and there was still a blue glow down along the edge of the glacier where the ice met the sky. I was on duty, doing a patrol with Charlie, but he had disappeared an hour or so ago. I had gotten too far behind and had lost sight of the tiny indents in the ice where his crampons had left their marks. The plan had been to climb Ptarmigan Ridge in a day, a route I'd never done before. Charlie had the map, but I should have known the way regardless. I yelled for a while to see if he could hear me, watching the sun get lower and lower while dusk fell over the green hills in the valley. I turned my light on, and then it was the only light.

Charlie always listened to music when he climbed, so he might not notice for hours that I was gone. When he did notice, I wasn't sure what he'd do. Maybe he'd come back, maybe he'd keep going. If he did come back, it would be good for me to be here, waiting. If he didn't come back, in the morning—early, before the snow got too soft—I'd hike back to the car. I didn't want to keep going up, not knowing if this was where the route went. I didn't know why I didn't know where the route went. I should have known. I wasn't scared, I could always hike back down, I was just sad that I'd been left.

A week later, after Charlie had come back and gotten angry with me, and then forgiven me for being slow, and crying, and not knowing the way, I realized that I was no longer trying to prove to the world that I could do my job. I was just trying to make it through each day without losing myself, hurting anyone, or going insane. The work was amazing, but there was too much of it. I enjoyed talking to the public about route conditions, staffing the high camps, and patrolling routes up the mountain. If someone got hurt on a route, I went there and made it turn out all right, but I only got a full night's sleep once every two or three nights. I fell asleep climbing, cooking, eating. My hands shook and my eye twitched all the time. I couldn't recover, and consequently I was not a good partner or friend, and as a further consequence I got left.

After this Charlie scheduled me for a backcountry patrol by myself, and in a way it was a relief. I still had to get from point A to point B, but if I took a break it didn't matter. If I couldn't think of anything to say, it was OK. I wanted to be a good partner—a big part of why I wanted to be here was because I wanted kinship—but I'd also become good at self-assessment, and I knew if I tried to climb with Charlie again I would only fail again. We jointly decided that we would both do better if I climbed alone again for a while.

I picked the Kautz route, which is on the southeast side of the mountain. None of us had climbed it for a while, and we needed to update the conditions report. In the pre-dawn I packed a sleeping bag, a little food, a quart of water, and my climbing tools. Nobody except one of the Paradise volunteers knew where I was going. There was no one else around to tell the morning I left, and no one who would care except Mike, since he was the one who checked out my accountability sheet proving I had done work. I could go as slowly as I wanted, because nobody would be expecting me. If there was an accident, I would be too far away to do anyone any good. In many ways it was a working vacation.

When I got to the trailhead it was cold and foggy. It wasn't windy, but it felt too cold to be August, even on the mountain. I put my running shoes on. I always hike in shoes late in the season, when the snow surface is firm enough. The boots stay in my pack until I have to put crampons on.

I hiked slowly up the trail through deep woods, heading for Comet Falls. Early in the season, the first miles of this hike—and several thousand feet of elevation gain—can be bypassed by hiking across the Nisqually Glacier from Paradise, but this late, the cross-over involves a lot of rockfall, and I was glad I had the time to hike the long trail from lower down.

I found out later that an aerospace engineering student on summer vacation had tried climbing the Kautz the day before I did. His ex-girlfriend was climbing with the guide service, but he didn't have the money to go with her. He didn't have the money for much, but he decided to climb anyway. He rented an ice ax but didn't have the funds for crampons, so he sharpened tent stakes and found a way to duct-tape them to his boots. He packed up a blanket and a can of beans.

I never did see him on the trail or on the route. With the fog we could have passed right next to each other, and never known it.

It was midmorning before I made it up to Van Trump Park. I came out of the woods and into the meadow, which had no sense of openness that day because I could only see about fifteen feet ahead of me through the thick clouds. There was a tent site under some trees in a bit of a flat spot. I sat down there on my pack, and rested my head on my knees for a while, keeping my nose warm. I didn't think about anything. I've discovered it's best not to think about the future—it'll happen anyway.

When I got up I could feel the cold soaking into my face and my stomach. I had to concentrate to get my hands to work, to do the buckles on my pack. The cold made my hands throb. I put my pack on and stuck my hands in my pockets, where I hoped they'd warm up again once I got moving.

The trail ended at Van Trump Park. There were two climbers' paths heading into the fog, and I wasn't sure which one I should take. I took the right one, for no reason. It petered out almost immediately, but I got out my map and compass and checked the direction and it looked about right, so I kept going. As I headed up, the fog only got thicker.

I don't think the engineering student had a map. He was relying on determination and conditions as he encountered them to tell him the best way to get up the route. Which is not much different from what I did. A map is just a safety in a world that is inherently unsafe.

The meadow was gone almost immediately, replaced by big rocks in loose sand as I went higher. It was difficult walking—with each step my foot sank down and slid back, losing ground. The sand built up in my shoes, feeling like sandpaper when I wiggled my cold toes. I kept going. I tried sticking to the sand and rocks for a while, but it was so tedious that I switched to the snow fingers, the very terminus of the glacier groping down between the rock ridges. The snow was very hard but it had large sun cups, concave bowls like waves in a kiddie pool, and the surface of the snow was gritty. I could walk on it as long as I centered my foot in each depression.

As the angle got steeper, I realized that if I lost my balance I would slide a long way. I started slipping frequently and was forced to keep crisscrossing back and forth, trying to find the deepest, most evenly spaced sun cups. I almost fell once, but caught myself by quick, energy-consuming body contortions—bloodying my fingernails on the slope as I slid. My heart was beating wildly and I was out of breath, but I didn't feel scared, just annoyed that I'd expended so much energy. Carefully, I walked back to the rocks and took my pack off, getting out my boots and crampons.

Fear is an interesting thing. I almost never feel afraid, but I do sometimes get a sense of impending doom, and it's almost always at the start of a trip that I know is going to be a disaster. Over time I've learned that it's best to verbalize this feeling to my climbing partners, if I have them. But I've also learned that the trip's momentum can take over so that gut instinct and logic are rarely heeded, to our later regret. On solo trips, though, when I've had that feeling I've always turned around. After all, what are we without partners in a crisis? I'm still convinced that a disaster among friends is more easily survivable and can knit you closer together. A disaster when you're alone is miserable and taxing at best. At worst, with the added psychological pain of being left, it's a death sentence.

I don't know if the engineering student felt afraid during his climb. He didn't have the equipment or the skills to ascend the route, so logically what he did was stupid, but it wasn't hubris that made him do it. He didn't think he could make it. Later we found the campsite he'd used all summer as a base for his hikes. He'd left a post-dated journal, the entries, written days before, describing what he knew would happen to him on this climb. He wrote about how hungry he was. How his clothing and blanket were inadequate. How he was going to die. I think he had the same instincts I had. He knew, and he went anyway.

Gritty frost on top of the ice stuck to the underside of my crampons. It got warmer as I went up until it was like a greenhouse in the fog, with the snow getting gloppy. Eventually, I started to get above the fog. The snow stuck in huge balls to the bottoms of my boots, and I'd slide down every time I took a step, before the steel spikes of my dull crampons eventually caught. I debated whether this was better than wearing my running shoes.

I could see the mountaintop every once in a while through a hole in the fog. It looked the same as it always does. Very there. Meanwhile, the angle of the slope I was on kicked back a little, which was nice. I didn't feel so precarious, and I was relieved to see that I was right where I wanted to be. I could see the ridge ahead of me where the two different starts to the Kautz route came together. It wasn't very far away, but it took me a long time to get there.

I finally made it out of the clouds and into the sun. Every few steps, I stopped to enjoy the heat on my back. It felt so good that all I wanted to do was sleep. I couldn't see anything below me because of the clouds, and there were no people, or evidence that people had ever been there. It was as if the whole human world didn't exist anymore.

I came up to the ridge, looking for a little waterfall I knew was there. I found it, then walked over loose rocks at the base of the fall and around a big rock on the ridge crest, and found some campsites lower down. Stashed in the rocks of the campsite I chose were two gallon containers of white gas, a few old pickets, and a broken camp stove. I took my pack off and angled it so my back sweat would dry off it, then took my boots off, and my socks, and propped them up in the sun. Finally I took off my pants and shirt, took my water bottle, and walked naked over to the waterfall to fill it up. I didn't treat the water, I just drank it. It was freezing, it tasted like clean gravel, and it made my teeth hurt.

I put my clothes back on at sundown. They were still damp and cold, but not soaking. I got into my sleeping bag and watched the sunset. I tried calling Charlie on the radio, but he didn't answer. I supposed he was climbing out of Camp Muir. Looking over I could see Muir, a tiny dot on the horizon across the glaciers. It was getting cold fast, and so I zipped up my sleeping bag, pulled the hood up, and tightened the strings so only my nose and one eye were exposed.

The stars started to come out, and the wind picked up. I wanted to watch the stars, there were so many that the whole sky was white and glowing, but the breeze blew gravel in my eyes, up my nose, and in my ears, and I had to stick my head entirely inside the bag to escape it. I didn't set an alarm. I should have, but I didn't because in a lot of ways I didn't want to climb. I just wanted to be too far away to help anyone for a little while. Just long enough for a little rest.

I'm not sure when the student might have passed by my campsite. Maybe he'd passed it without a second thought. Or maybe he had camped there just the night before, and checked to see if the little stove jammed behind the rocks worked—thinking for a few moments about how nice some hot water would be, but then realizing it was a false hope—just like I did.

It was five AM before I got up. I couldn't stand the thought of eating another Snickers bar, so I ate an Emergen-C, the orange-flavored drink mix, like pop rocks for breakfast, straight from the package with no water. It left me foaming at the mouth. I stuffed my damp sleeping bag back into my backpack, and put my boots and crampons on. Then I took one of my two ice tools off the back of the pack, put the pack on, and started working the stiffness out of my legs.

I was tired, and knew that today I had to be slow and consistent. I was worried that the snowbridges over the crevasses higher on the route would be too soft later in the day. Too soft meant I'd fall through into a crevasse and die and nobody would ever find my body, but I hadn't wanted to get up any earlier than I had because a person who doesn't get enough sleep starts to go peculiar, which also can lead to dire results. I started up the mountain an hour after dawn, at first wearing my jacket, but after a few minutes I took it off. The wind had died down and it was going to be a bluebird day. Even the clouds in the valley were gone.

After about an hour I came around a big rock and saw a tent with three men standing around, drinking coffee. "Hi, I'm Bree, I'll be your park ranger today. Y'all having a good time?" They weren't. They had climbed this route a few days previously, but had been too scared to come back down the ice chute at the top of the route, so they had gone down a different way, and then hiked back up here from the parking lot in order to get the camp they'd left. I thought they were burly to come back and get their camp. Most people would have just left it. I'd found perfectly set up camps long abandoned here before, full of new gear. Fortunes of war. Funny how we compare mountain climbing to war, when mountain climbing is something people do for fun.

I left them drinking coffee next to their tents and continued on. I had to climb down below the Kautz ice cliff, a large hanging ice fall. As the day warmed up, the ice cracked. The fall loomed above me, a huge blue art-deco death-trap. I crossed this section at a steady pace. I absolutely didn't want to linger here, but at the same time I didn't want to move too fast and wear myself out completely. I emerged on the other side and for the first time looked up at the ice chute above the cliff. It didn't look too steep. Early in the season, the chute is just steepish snow, but as the season progresses it gets icier and icier until finally it's a sixty-degree slope of water-ice, a clear blue you can see deep down into. I stood below it for a while, knowing I should move on and get this part over with. Looking down at the foot of the glacier, way, way below me, I was happy for the first time in a long while. There weren't any distractions. There was just me here, and I only had one thing that I could do, go up. Simple as survival.

I don't know if the engineering student ever was here at the ice cliff above Camp Hazard. In his post-dated diary, he wrote that on the second day he would be climbing hard ice, but it would be too much for his skills and his homemade equipment. He said that he would fall and slide, tumbling and bloody, into a crevasse. He wouldn't die at first, he imagined, but too injured to get out, he would lie there at the bottom for a long time.

I took my other ice tool off my pack and started up the ice.

It felt steeper than sixty degrees, I think because I was alone. My pack felt heavy, but I knew it wasn't. The only things in it were my lightest sleeping bag; half a quart of water; a few Snickers bars; a jacket; map and compass; and a pair of running shoes.

It had been really cold for a long time prior to my climb, and the ice was brittle. When I hit it with my ax, huge chunks split off that would dinner-plate out and hit me in the face, or the knees, or land on my feet, threatening to jar my crampons out of the ice. Sometimes on this section there were huge penetentes, like large misshapen stalagmite formations, that you could hang onto or lean against for a rest, but this time there were none. I kept visualizing myself ripping back down the ice in a wild fall, somersaulting down and over the cliff at the bottom. I had seen what this spot had done to other people. I did not feel invincible. There are some places where a person cannot afford to sneeze, and on this day, for me, this was one of them.

I couldn't get my tools to stick in the ice. It was too brittle. I was afraid that the chunks splitting off would knock me off completely. My hold was too precarious for me to try putting the tools back on my pack, so I left them hanging from my wrists where they caught on every irregularity in the ice. For stability, I put my hands on the ice in front of me and continued climbing with just the frontpoints of my crampons in the ice, a quarter-inch of two metal spikes barely angled in to keep me from dying.

To complicate things, there were huge holes in the ice, dark chasms with thin little walls that I had to step on, step up on, try not to fall into. I was listening to my MP3 player. To the Black Eyed Peas's "Anxiety." The player was in my pocket, and every time I high-stepped my thigh would press the volume button higher. I couldn't stop to fix it, so the music in my ears got unbearably loud in the silent glacial world. When I stopped for a moment, my calves started to shake. The climbing wasn't that difficult, and

I couldn't figure out why my muscles were flaming out except that I was being too careful, and needed to move faster.

Finally, I came to the top of the ice. I wanted to throw up, I was so tired. I turned the music down. There was a flat spot. It was late in the morning and I needed to keep going, but I sat down on my pack and ate another candy bar, drank the rest of my water, and then just sat in the sun. It was a fairly flat glacier, gently angling upward above the ice chute. On its surface were several huge round ice blobs that seemed to have come from out of nowhere—they looked like giant snowballs, left randomly. The nearest one was about fifteen feet high. I walked over to it without my pack, climbed to the top of it, and looked around. The view was exactly the same as it had been on the glacier, except for when I looked straight down.

The student spent his summer break illegally camping and hiking through the park, looking at crazy things. I hope he somehow made it up above the chute to see the snow blobs.

It was now very late in the morning, the snow was getting soft, and my feet were sinking six inches or more with every step. There were huge crevasses everywhere with late-season, sagging snowbridges crossing over them like a giant maze, and with every minute the bridges were getting more unstable.

I started walking again. There was a rock ridge I could stay on for a while, but then I had to cross another glacier which was very broken with crevasses. I could only guess which way to go through.

Some of the crevasses were massive, a hundred or more feet across, with the lip on the far side hung with huge icicles, and each end disappearing into the snow. I never wanted to cross the snow too close to the crevasse edge, since it was thin there, but I didn't want to waste time or energy walking too far around, either. Several times, one of my feet punched through the snow and into the edge of a crevasse, or maybe into the middle of another crevasse I couldn't see. I was getting hazard pay for this, a couple of dollars an hour extra.

You can never tell how thick the snow covering a crevasse will be. I always stopped falling after one foot or both feet went in because the additional surface area provided by my crotch, my ass, or at least my backpack when they hit the surface of the snow spread out my weight enough so I didn't break all the way through into a bottomless abyss. When I felt myself start to fall, I instinctively put my arms straight out—something I'd seen mellow drunks do back in my days driving an ambulance. We used to call it the Jesus Position. Maybe I did it so I wouldn't fall in—not that I actually thought my arms would be long enough to span crevasses that were easily fifty feet across. Maybe I did it in case I did break all the way through, for the reason the drunks did it, surrendering myself to whatever came next.

Higher up, I got to a weird spot. As far as I could see in either direction, an enormous crevasse cut across my path. Its edges were overhung, and I could hear water running down into its dark blue everlasting. I could see a few snowbridges across it, but they were all drooping even without my extra weight on them.

There was only one that I thought I could cross. It rose up like a bridge, twisted in the middle, and came down on the far side—looking like the McDonald's arch with a twist at the top. I didn't want to cross it, but I knew I was going to have to. I wanted someone to know where I was in case I fell in. If I died on the mountain I wanted my body to stay there, but I didn't want my friends to have to look for me forever.

I tried calling Charlie on the radio again, and this time he answered. I told him which glacier I was on, and that I would give him a call back in fifteen minutes, which was about the amount of time I thought it would to take me to get across the bridge. He wanted to know why I was calling, and I said I would be down to

Camp Muir in a bit and I just wanted to know if he was there. I looked around again. It had been nice to talk to somebody, but now I had a deadline.

The bridge creaked and I was petrified crawling across it, but I spent a moment more than I should have at the apex, looking down into the crevasse. The view was crazy. Like looking into a black hole trying to suck me in. I could feel the entity of the living glacier inhale, the warm air rush past me into the shadow, pulling at me, and then I was on the other side.

I decided not to try to summit the mountain. The top is only the top, and I couldn't care less anymore. I hadn't cared for a long time. I needed to get to Muir, and it was all about the shortest distance between two points. The Ingraham Glacier was very broken, and I had to cross it before I could meet up with the popular Disappointment Cleaver route that would take me down to camp.

By now it was afternoon and the snow was getting even softer. With each step I was sinking almost to my knees, but somehow the snow I'd stuffed into my water bottle hadn't melted at all. Such is life. Every time I sank into the snow, I wondered whether my foot would stop, or break through the ceiling of another crevasse and wave around in nothingness. I was thirsty, but I had to continue going up, within five hundred feet of the summit, in order to find a way through the crevasses. Mine were the only footprints.

It was early afternoon when I hit the DC. The DC is a trail packed down two feet wide; the guide service maintains it with shovels. It was nice to go downhill. There was nobody else this high on the mountain so late in the day. I kept catching my crampons on my pant cuffs, and every time I would almost fall. I laughed at myself a little bit, and was glad no one was there to see me stumble. I had to jump across a few crevasses on the way down, but I did it without breaking stride—I had to have some small skill.

Coming into Ingraham Flats I passed two climbers who were

also headed down. I said, "Hi," and asked them if they were do-ing OK. They looked tired and grumpy. They said they'd been out climbing since eleven o'clock the night before, but they'd made the summit. I congratulated them, and added that if they wanted to come by the ranger station later there might be margaritas. They said that sounded nice, but they said it wistfully, like the idea was a mirage of a watering hole when they were lost forever in the desert. I kept going.

I paused at the top of Cathedral Gap to fix my hair and make sure I didn't have any more gravel in my teeth, and then I cruised down into camp. Charlie was sleeping, but he woke up when I walked into the hut.

I kept more food at Camp Muir than all the other rangers combined. Besides the margarita mix (excellent with a little te-quila and late-summer corn snow) I was planning on cooking up some phad thai with a real lime, peanuts, and tinned chicken, but it wasn't meant to be. Charlie sent me immediately on to Para-dise, to get ready for another two-day climbing patrol starting first thing in the morning. I hid the lime away and refilled my water bottle, though water was scarce at Muir and I was headed to a kitchen full of faucets. I didn't care, I was thirsty. I took my boots off and put my running shoes back on, and then shuffled off the deck, trying not to look too stiff.

That next patrol never did happen. I returned to Paradise, into the beginning of what became a heavily funded and manpow-er intensive incident covered by a media firestorm. The next five days I spent searching the same route I'd just covered, looking for the missing student. He was never found.

8

THREE DAYS

IT WAS ALMOST SEPTEMBER. Little ice pellets were bouncing everywhere over Camp Muir: over the gravel helipad in the middle of camp, over the walkways and the stone stairs we'd shored up again and again in the sandy hill, over the deck that smelled like piss because nobody wanted to walk all the way to the outhouse in the middle of the night, over the crusty black snow that had been melting around us all year.

I walked outside into the cold, and felt the hail landing in my hair and running down behind my ears. Everything was gray, everywhere I looked. There were clouds above me, clouds below me, and clouds between the buildings. I ambled down the stairs to the outhouse. It was starting to get windy and it would be dark soon, in a little less than two hours. The lingering day trippers needed to get going to make it back to Paradise before dark.

I sloshed some straight bleach around the toilet seat. Rich, Ted's boss and the head of the backcountry buildings and outhouses department, wanted us to dilute it to save money, but the only bucket we could dilute it in was our dishpan. I didn't want to take the dishpan anywhere near the outhouse.

I noticed that the basket under the seat needed to be changed.

Under the toilet seat are six baskets down below in a box. The baskets hold the shit, and this basket was full to within a foot of the seat. I really didn't want to rotate it out today. I had another two days up here, without any way to clean myself up, and the job was impossible to do without getting shit on the sleeves of my jacket. I didn't want to be dirty that long; it was disgusting. I decided the project could wait another day.

That was a good decision, because Rich radioed just then saying that a contract helicopter would be at Muir in thirty minutes, and I needed to haul a bunch of man-sized propane tanks to the helipad so they'd be ready to fly out before it got here. They were too heavy to lift, so I dragged them all up and down the stairs across camp as fast as I could. Most of the tanks had been lined up on top of the slab behind the outhouse where the pans under the baskets drain, so the bottoms were rusted out with rain, piss, and who knows what else.

It was a hot job despite the weather, and I'd taken my jacket off and left it mid-run, between the ranger hut and the helipad, on a big rock. When I finally finished, I came back for my jacket but it was gone. I couldn't believe it. People don't steal things from Muir. None of the guides, climbers, or day hikers claimed to have seen it. I sat down on the rock with my back aching, and stared out at the clouds. I felt the day slipping into the negative. It would be all downhill from here.

It was a devastating loss. I only had two warm jackets, and wore one on top of the other. In bad weather, I wore a waterproof jacket on top of both. I wouldn't be able to replace the lost jacket until my next days off, and it would cost a couple of days' wages. I could feel the insidious cold, my enemy, already pressing against my back.

Tired of feeling sorry for myself, I wrestled all the tanks, along with my cooking garbage that I didn't want to pack out, onto a big net on the gravel helipad. I was happy now for the heavy labor, glad for the heat I was producing and for the physical and painful work I could pour my frustrations into. I shooed all the day trippers off the edge of the pad, saying the helicopter would be there in a few minutes. It wasn't true. I could tell there would be no flights here today—the clouds were too thick, it was too windy. I didn't care. I was angry, my voice had an edge to it, I wanted to exercise the full extent of my small authority over these jacket-stealers—the authority granted by my Park Service hat, the only official thing I had on. I was as cold as the cold. We were one.

Looking down through the clouds, I saw a bunch of kids roughhousing on the glacier below Muir. The average climber at Muir is a middle-aged man, so children romping on the glacier was a bit unusual. And this late in the season, during a low snow year, it was scary. They didn't know what I knew—namely, that below camp were a lot of crevasses overhung with thin snow edges that would collapse under body weight and send an un-suspecting victim plunging down into a hundred feet of slimy black ice. As I thought about it, I wanted to experience it: it fit my mood, suffocating alone in the blackness of this uncaring mountain. Still, I had my job to do.

I found a man who was attached to the kids, sitting on a rock, and leaning against the side of the guide service's bunkhouse, a creosote-covered plywood box that looked like it should have blown away years ago. The man was bent over with his hands in his armpits, trying to stay out of the wind. He was wearing an inad-equate, thin nylon sports jacket and didn't have any kind of pack with him. His nose was purple.

"Hi," I said, "I'm Bree, the ranger up here on duty this afternoon. Are those your kids?" I pointed in a sweeping gesture to encompass the six or so kids, barely visible because of the hail, who were wres-tling in the snow and sliding down the shallow incline towards the nearest of the gaping crevasses. I paused, squinting into the haze, trying to pick out details. The girls wore long flannel dresses and bonnets. Both girls and boys were soaking wet, covered with hail and the cruddy summer snow.

"Some of them are mine," the man said, unwilling to look up at me because it would mean moving his chin out of the paltry warmth of his jacket.

"Well," I lied, "it's going to be dark soon, and so I'm just letting everybody know that now is probably a good time to start heading back down the hill." As much as I believe in personal responsibility and learning from your mistakes, I was seeing a lot of suffering in this group's near future once they quit horsing around and realized that it was snowing and windy, that they didn't have any dry clothes, and that they were a long way from home. I thought maybe they needed a nudge towards enlightenment.

There was a long pause and the hail fell like BBs over us. I stood silently with my hands in my pants pockets, waiting for the response I wanted. If I didn't get it, I would start with the strong-arm stuff. I didn't know what I could do really, but I wasn't above anything today.

"Yeah," the man said, finally, "we should probably get a move on. Most of our group didn't make it all the way up to Muir, and they're waiting for us a little ways down."

"Ahh," I said, "well, have a good trip." I said it warmly, and it was the only warmth there was.

I got another radio call from Rich. Flights were cancelled because the weather was getting worse. "OK," I said. The propane tanks could sit where they were on the pad until tomorrow. I didn't want to be outside anymore today, I wanted a cup of tea and my sleeping bag.

It had been a hard week already. My climbing boots had blown out, so the only footwear I had with me were my running shoes. I'd duct-taped a pair of flimsy aluminum crampons onto them for the unreasonably large stretches of ice that had suddenly appeared above Pan Point, halfway to Muir from Paradise. I worried that someone would need help on the upper mountain, and I really didn't want to go up there by myself in this storm, small as it was, with just running shoes. Sometimes climbing the mountain in running shoes isn't so bad, but a protracted rescue in cold footwear means frostbite and, personal injury aside, if my boss saw me I'd be fired. Two climbing rangers had fallen and died because of poor-quality footwear, and there was now a no-tolerance policy.

A few weeks before, the park superintendent's personal aide, Randy, had asked me what kind of boots I used on the mountain. I hesitated, and then told him my boots were not actually very good, but that I was saving up to get the pair I needed. I asked him a lot of questions about his feet and gave him some good suggestions for the type of boots he needed, since we all knew he and the superintendent were planning on climbing the mountain sometime during the summer. We had a nice chat, but Randy talked to Mike about my boot crisis, and Mike sat me down and told me that any time I needed gear, I only had to come talk to him, not blab to the whole park. He had actually promised new boots for all the climbing rangers, a nice gesture because the park wasn't obligated to provide us with equipment, but the money ran out once the north side rangers had gotten theirs. Politics. I admonished myself to learn to keep quiet.

I climbed the stairs back to the ranger hut, the Butt Hut—affectionately nicknamed for a ranger named William Butler and unfortunately descriptive of its general appearance and odor. It wasn't any warmer inside the tiny plywood hut than it was outside. When I tried to put water on for tea, I found that the stove wasn't working. One of the two propane tanks we used had been empty and I'd taken it to the helipad to be flown out, but I realized now there was no shut-off valve between the two tanks, so when

I turned the propane on the good tank on, the gas only hissed out the empty side of the connector. Damn. No stove to melt snow for water or to make tea.

It was going to be harder than I'd thought to warm myself up. I'd boxed up all the extra jackets and three of the four sleeping bags to be flown down for their yearly cleaning. They were communal sleeping bags, slept in every night all summer by a variety of sweaty, hairy, chili-eating rangers. I pulled off my wet running shoes and got into the remaining bag with all my clothes on for a nap and to try to warm up. It was hard to sleep with frozen feet, knowing they were down there at the end of the cot, jammed up against the wall all white and wet and wrinkled. I tried wiggling my toes, and most of them responded. Maybe things weren't so bad, even though I was curled up in a fetal position, almost incapacitated by violent shivering.

About ten minutes later the guide service started calling Camp Muir. They had to call a few times before they got my attention. The sound of the radio was muffled through the sleeping bag and there was also, like every day, a steady stream of radio traffic from the law enforcement rangers reading out license plate numbers in the parking lots and on park roads for background checks: "I'm rolling·east on 123 at milepost 16 with yankee, bravo, blah, blah, blah, comes back clear and valid to a Mr. Goodman out of Enumclaw, blah, blah, blah."

I tried to answer the guide service in a lull, but the communications center cut me off for interrupting, reminding me that law enforcement traffic takes precedence on the radio because their jobs are dangerous and their communication link vital.

I waited, feeling my fingers stiffen around the radio mike. Eventually, the conversation ended, the tag was clear and valid, the case number confirmed. RMI said they were coming up the mountain with a bunch of clients. They were currently at nine thousand feet and had just passed a group of sixteen people, mostly children, who were unable to get down the mountain because they were afraid of falling on the ice. All of them were wet and hypothermic.

I burrowed into the sleeping bag, stretching the mike cord. This was just fantastic. I was sure it was my group from earlier, and they'd only made it down a thousand feet, a fifth of the way to Paradise. I thanked RMI for letting me know, and said I'd go get them. I laid there a moment longer with my eyes closed. I still couldn't feel my feet, I was spent, I let out a long high-pitched whine like a dog.

I wished there was another ranger here so we could laugh about the ludicrousness of sixteen people in bonnets loose on the snowfield. We could groan together; it would be a funny story to tell later, with our audience bent over, unable to breathe, with tears in their eyes. It was a tragedy there was no one else here.

Finally, I loosened the drawcord on the sleeping bag and reached up for the cell phone that worked as long as my head was at the right angle. I called the Paradise dorm, hoping some of my coworkers would be there. Adrienne answered.

"Hey," I said. "There's this big group of, uh, you know I think they're Amish people, sixteen of them, mostly kids. RMI just called me and said they're stuck at nine thousand feet, and they don't have crampons or anything to get down the ice, they're hypothermic and not moving. I guess I'm going to go down there and see what I can do for them, but if you could call Stefan and ask him if he'd hire one of the volunteers just to bring up some more dry clothes and help me corral these guys down, it would be real nice."

"OK," said Adrienne. "Call me back in about ten minutes." I unzipped the sleeping bag and felt the whoosh of all the moist, warm air escape in a steam cloud, instantly replaced by bone-chilling dampness. I put my shoes back on. Thankfully, they weren't frozen yet, but there was water bubbling out the toes. I drank the last of my Gatorade, then called Adrienne back.

"Nope, he won't allow it, he says there's not enough money left in the budget to pay anybody overtime, or hire any volunteers even for a few hours, especially if it isn't a real emergency. Have fun, though," she said, giggling. "Glad it's you and not me."

"Thanks for trying, Adrienne." This was my third summer as a climbing ranger on the mountain, but for the life of me I couldn't understand what constituted an emergency and what didn't. I'd seen legions dispatched for a dizzy person in the meadows on a midsummer day, inordinate numbers requisitioned for broken legs, hundreds involved in hopeless body recoveries, but help rarely seemed available when I needed it. When help did come, I was second-guessed later: I was weak for having asked. I didn't understand it, because as a personal philosophy I like containment, a backup plan, a partner for safety's sake. I resolved to keep asking for help no matter how weak it made me look.

I filled my pack with ice axes and a first-aid kit, and grabbed a handful of Snickers bars for my pockets. Almost right out of camp, I had to put my crampons on. I'd never seen the snowfield so icy. It was deep blue ice with runnels of water becoming moulons, huge rivers running swiftly over the glacier in progressively deeper troughs until finally they plunged through black holes deep into the glacier. These things eat people.

I couldn't get my crampons adjusted small enough for my running shoes—I needed to drill a new hole further down the bar, but I hadn't had time. With every step, my foot slid about an inch forward to the end of the crampon, my toes bashing into the front bail. Then, when I lifted up my foot, it made a slapping sound, like walking in flip-flops. It was the only noise besides my breathing and the hiss of the hail that continued to fall.

Visibility was terrible, and I was afraid of missing the group altogether, so I zigzagged back and forth across the slope hoping to see them. Finally, I found them huddled together on a little rock knoll. It was the group from before, but they'd apparently met up with the rest of their party, which was a good thing because now I didn't have to look for the other half, too.

"Hi," I said. "I'm Bree, the ranger up here. You guys want to get out of here?" I stood before them hugging myself, trying to keep the heat trapped in my one remaining warm jacket.

"You're it?" said one woman with a huge bosom. "We asked for help, and you're IT?"

I realized I was going to have to change my posture. I stood up straight, palms out, and started gesturing. "I'm not so bad," I said, smiling, "I know the way down, and I've brought chocolate bars." I pulled the king-size Snickers bars out of my pockets, and started waving them enticingly, though looking at the crowd of them I added, "You might have to share."

The woman glared at me. I wondered if she knew I wasn't getting paid for this. I wondered if she knew that if I wasn't there, she'd probably freeze to death, or fall in a moulon and then freeze to death. The group was much too far west of the main trail to make it down. Without a major course correction, they'd end up cliffed out in the dark in the middle of a hailstorm. I wondered why she still managed to make me feel defensive, like apologizing for showing up.

I looked around. The women and girls wore, in addition to the bonnets and dresses, high-heeled lace-up boots with no tread on the soles. I opened my pack and handed out my hat, my one pair of gloves, and my waterproof jacket, one each, to three of the kids. They were all shivering and glassy-eyed. Some of them were a little bloody on the chins and elbows from previous spills, and they all looked disinclined to continue, some of them lying in an all-too-familiar fetal position on the ground between the rocks.

I took off my one remaining jacket and gave it to a little boy who couldn't have been more than four, leaving me with only my still-damp synthetic T-shirt.

"It's not enough," said the woman flatly. There were nine young children in the group, all of whom were still obviously freezing, not to mention all the adults, and now me, too. "It'll be fine," I said. "Once we get moving, everybody'll warm up. Let's go, quick."

"I can't go," the woman replied, almost mocking me, trying to be ornery. "I sprained my ankle in a fall, and now I can't walk on it."

I looked off into the distance, thinking, *We have to go now, we have to go now, we have to go now.* I looked her in the eye and said, "Well, if you stay, you'll freeze to death, and since you're choosing to stay, it's suicide, and can you really get into heaven that way?" I hoped there was some sort of religious background associated with the bonnets that I could guilt her with. "Here, I'll look at your ankle real quick."

I took her boot off and she was only wearing nylons. Her ankle was slightly blue. I wrapped an ace bandage around it and shoved her boot back on as fast as I could with frozen fingers. The men were sitting slightly separately, We didn't speak to each other, although they looked at me every once in a while.

Then I stood up. "OK, let's go."

I handed out the ice axes, saying, "These are short walking sticks, use them to keep your balance, and if you start to slide, let it go." I figured that this was a fine tutorial in this case, since it was probably too icy to arrest a fall in any case. A few of them asked if I had any water, and nobody was pleased when I said there was a drinking fountain in Paradise. Two other women helped support the busty one, one on each side, and I was grateful for their help.

I put my empty pack on the four-year-old and let him ride pig-gyback. We started out with the rest of the children trailing silently behind me. It was slow going, and even more difficult because the men would go too far ahead, always in the wrong direction. I would yell at them to wait for the rest of us, but I think they couldn't understand why the ranger couldn't keep up with them. They kept yelling back that if I thought I needed to lead them, then I needed to stay in the front, otherwise I wasn't helping. Finally, tired of yelling, I just took my own way and hoped they'd look back every once in a while and change direction with me.

It was hard to see anything and I had to keep my compass out around my neck, checking it constantly to make sure we were still somewhat on track.

It got dark. We made an impressive group, weaving down the mountain. Mine was the only light, and then there was a line of shadows trailing me. As we got lower, it got warmer and started sleeting. It was so foggy I couldn't tell if everybody was still together or not, but I thought it would be hopeless to try counting again and again.

When we finally got to Pan Point, the glacier ended and we were back on the trails, two-thirds of the way back to Paradise. The men and some of the faster kids took off then, stumbling in the dark, unwilling to wait for the large woman and her cohort. I gave them directions on what trails to take, and hoped they remembered the order. The rest of us made it back to the parking lot in the middle of the night, soaked and freezing, but alive and together. The kid I'd given my jacket to had had a bowel control problem in it, and he'd also somehow ripped the zipper off.

The rest of the group were waiting at their cars, angry that we'd taken so long. Apparently, there was an issue with who had the car keys. I figured they'd tell me if anyone was missing. I asked for my hat and gloves and raincoat back, and waited a long time in the rain, holding my soiled jacket, standing outside their bank of vehicles while they changed inside them. The kids finally threw my things out the fogged-up windows, where they landed in puddles—which didn't make them any wetter. I thanked everyone and walked off into the dark, back to the dorm. I couldn't handle going back up to Muir just yet.

I wondered what the group would think about the experience, if they ever thought about it. I wondered if they'd complain. I wondered what would happen to me if they complained. Some of them, especially the vocal woman, were pretty angry at the delays, and the lack of support, and that I hadn't had more lights, and chocolate, and clothes. I don't know. I mean, what did they want from me? It's true that they paid to get into the park, and that money is supposed to cover emergency services, and I was a pathetic thing to hold up under the heading "emergency services."

But it was the middle of the night, I wasn't getting paid, I was going to have to buy more chocolate bars, and I was out two jackets in one day. I also needed to start back up to Muir, because I needed to get back to my post in case something else happened.

I didn't go back up. I couldn't leave the dorm. I felt like a failure and an embarrassment, and the self-pity was paralyzing. Everybody was asleep and it was warm inside, and the kitchen light was glowing, inviting. I peeled off all my wet clothes to take a shower and turned the water up as hot as it would go, hot enough so that I had to turn in tight circles to keep from scalding any one part of myself. I stayed in until all my skin turned red. It was almost four AM when I crawled into bed and set the alarm for six.

In the morning I rolled out of bed, feeling old, dizzy, and weak. I put on the same clothes from the previous day, and halfway through I remembered that my lightweight hi-tech alpine jackets were no more. Casting around for replacements, I pulled on my green park-issue uniform jacket and then struggled into my dressy out-on-the-town jacket. The result was bulky and odd looking, but warm enough. I walked to the kitchen, refilled my water bottle, and threw in two scoops of orange-flavored Gatorade powder. I opened the freezer and checked out my breakfast options. There was a huge stack of Eggos and nothing else. I pulled out eight and popped them two at a time into the toaster oven to eat and then repeat.

I started hiking at six-thirty. I didn't want anyone to know I had spent the night in Paradise. The truth is, I could have made it back up to Muir, but I was lulled by the twin sirens of bed and hot water, and I was too weak to refuse. I couldn't figure out what was wrong with me. I was supposed to love climbing and live for the thrill of every second I could be out on the mountain. Charlie worked hard to give me as much time on the mountain as he could, away from the office and the meaningless stacks of government forms. I was grateful, but . . . there was no but. I needed to be grateful, and beyond grateful, I needed to love it. "I love this," I said to the fog outside the front door.

The truth was, I did love it. In my first season I spent a three-day patrol hiking from Longmire to climb Success Cleaver with another ranger. It was remote enough that no other climbers ever ventured there and the alpine meadows and views from the Cleaver were the best I'd ever seen on the mountain.

I enjoyed helping folks, too. The previous year, one day when a friend was staying with me at Muir, I got a call at about five in the afternoon about a stranded party on the Cleaver. We decided to go up and see what the problem was, and if there wasn't a problem, we'd just keep going and do a sunset climb. We found the stranded party, a group of marines who had spend the last eight hours sitting on the Cleaver staring at their map, but they refused to take route suggestions from a girl in pigtails and Patagonia Hawaiian flower print shorts (I was off duty). I said fine, we were going to summit, and if they changed their minds they could follow us back down when we returned in a few hours—which was what eventually happened. It had been great fun.

Sometimes even just being at Muir was good. We used to melt our water there in a sixty-gallon black plastic garbage can we'd set on the south side of the deck in the sun. The water did get a bit gunky and silty at the bottom, but as long as we used water off the top and added snow every time we took water out, we had a constant water supply that rarely froze up completely. At least, it worked well until one day at the very end of the summer, when the ice block that was always floating on the top finally melted. Charlie and I realized, to our horror and amusement, that a mouse had drowned in it and had probably been slowly decomposing in our water supply for several months. That was the only year we used the garbage can. We took a picture of the corpse and stuck it on our fridge in Paradise.

But I was alone too much. I needed a real partner in crime, someone to play off of, so we could motivate each other, share stories and have each other's backs.

The weather was getting better. I hiked past the few late-season flowers in the dying meadows, past the brown heather between the rocks, up into the snow. It wasn't warm enough to stop moving this early in the morning, and I only paused momentarily, just above Pebble Creek, to put my aluminum crampons back on my running shoes. None of us had needed crampons to get to Muir until this fall, and I think there was a bit of a stigma about using them. I'd seen some of the guides going without them and I'd tried it a few times, but for me it was faster to wear them and deal with the potential humiliation than to slide backward every couple of steps. I wanted the trip to be mindless. I just wanted to get there.

I looked up. It was definitely clearing up—still overcast, but the clouds were high. and I could see all the way to the lenticular cloud swirling on the summit. I always thought these clouds seemed like living things, blasting around like the Fates dancing.

When I finally got back to the Butt Hut, it was after ten. My fingers were cold, and it was hard to open the combination lock on the door. Inside the hut was messy, my food strewn everywhere from yesterday's search for good things to eat that didn't have to be cooked. Still standing in the doorway, I turned around and squinted at the campground. There were a few tents out there. I hadn't had time to do rounds last night, so I didn't know who was out climbing and who wasn't. I hoped anyone who'd gone would come back soon without incident.

I closed the door and stood in the middle of the hut for a minute, shivering and hunched over. My mind completely numb, I stared at the lighter from the Paradise Inn gift shop I'd left on the counter. "I love this," I said aloud. "I love this, I love this, I love this." I went back to staring at the lighter. It had a tiny white outline of the mountain on one side.

I remembered that there was an emergency hiking stove, a beat-on little thing, which I found and quickly assembled on the countertop. It wasn't supposed to be used indoors, because it produced carbon monoxide, which can build up to toxic levels and kill people in confined spaces. The hut had had a carbon monoxide alarm, but it went off every time we cooked on the regular stove, and half the time otherwise, so finally we threw it out and vowed to keep the door open a crack when we cooked.

I threw a huge pot of ice on top of the single-burner stove. It wobbled a bit, but stayed on. It would take a few hours for the water to melt.

Right after I put it on, Rich called and told me that flights were back on for the day. He was also sending up some equipment, and wanted to make sure there was a clear place to drop it off. A construction crew was remodeling the public shelter that summer—they had only a few weeks to do it between peak climbing season and winter—and right where the equipment needed to go were two and a half pallets of concrete.

The helicopter was minutes away, so I grabbed the construction folks. They were an odd couple amid the black Gore-Tex and bright beanie-clad climbers in the campground: he a blond Nordic god with a huge beak nose, always decked out in overalls and a handknit blue sweater; she tromping about in knee-high rubber barn boots and braided pigtails. We moved all the concrete over about six feet as fast as we could, bag by eighty-pound bag, running and stumbling with the bags, tripping over each other, and laughing. It felt fantastic to have the company. By the time we were finished it was getting windier, and I started to doubt if the flight would go.

I walked back to the Butt Hut. The stove had gone out. I pumped the fuel bottle to repressurize the line and grabbed the lighter. Rich called and said that flights had been cancelled again because of the weather. We'd try it again next week. "OK," I said.

I needed to rotate the baskets in the outhouses, but the wind was going to make it difficult. As soon as I would open the back of the box, used toilet paper would fly around in the wind. There were separate receptacles in the outhouses for toilet paper, but a lot of people didn't use them, instead tossing the paper down the hole.

We had white Tyvex moon suits to use when we dumped the filled baskets into sixty-gallon barrels that were flown off the mountain every week or so, but the suits were too expensive to use every time the baskets got rotated. So I just had to be careful when I leaned way in, with my head between the underside of the toilet seat hole and the top of the full basket, in order to heave the heavy basket over. I was tempted to put my elbows on the edge of the waist-high pan or to press up against it to get more leverage against the basket, but the whole edge was covered with dried human shit, and because I was wearing my out-on-the-town coat this time, I really didn't want to touch anything. I pulled on my latex exam gloves, held my breath, and headed in.

At least there weren't any flies at Muir. No animal life made it up this high. Sometimes a bird or mouse spent a day or two, and then moved on. Twenty years ago, I was told, a whole cloud of monarch butterflies had been blown in during a storm, and they covered everything so thickly that they dripped from the eaves of the buildings. That would have been something to see.

I walked around the front of the outhouse and peered down the hole to see if the new basket was centered under the toilet seat. Close enough. It sucked when shit spooged down and then dried onto the basket handles.

The stove had gone out again. I pumped up the fuel bottle and relit the stove. The ice was starting to melt, now it was a floating block with an inch of water around the edge. I decided it was enough to make lunch. I heated up a can of "just add water" soup, and made some tea along with it. The soup was gritty from silt, but it was hot and really, really nice. I fancied that it would be fabulous with some additional carrots and onions, and maybe some corn and mushrooms and some vegetable broth. Maybe a nice rosemary potato bread and butter, warm of course.

I left the lunch pot outside next to the door, put the water pot back on the stove, and gave the fuel bottle a few more pumps. It was afternoon. After the warm meal and my late night, I was really sleepy. All I wanted was to lie down for a minute or two.

I looked at my watch, and it was only three. It was cold and dreary outside, and cold and lonely inside. Somebody had broken the antenna off the little FM radio and it wasn't working. The drawl of the law enforcement rangers on the Park Service radio was hypnotic: "Foxtrot, sierra, charlie, papa, copy?"

I couldn't help it. I had to nap. I pulled the drawcord tight on the greasy fartsack so only my nose was sticking out. My joints ached, and my shirt and socks were still soaked from the trip up that morning. I'd picked up a layer of dust from the concrete and it had become mud on my black climbing pants. The sleeping bag was still damp at the bottom from yesterday's wet socks. I curled up . . . and there was a knock on the door. "Come in," I yelled from inside the bag.

The door opened. I moved the hole from my nose to one eye. I could see a silhouette of a man with a lot of jackets on. He looked humpy and tired. Behind him I could see the clouds were starting to break up. There were patches of blue, but no sun yet. "Lazy days," the man said, eyeing me back.

"Yeah," I replied, struggling to find the drawcord again and stick my head out. "Late season and all that. I'm Bree, I really am the ranger on duty up here today. What can I do for ya?"

"Nothing," he said. "But my group just got down from the summit." There was a pause while the man let me digest the awesome fact that he had just summitted the mountain. I'm sure my facial features gave away that I remained unfazed.

"Anyway, on our way down we were behind this group of three guys, who hadn't summitted,"—there was another pause, and then he continued—"when these huge ice chunks let loose from the Direct right next to the toe of the Cleaver. I mean right at them. We yelled and they yelled and ran, but it totally smashed into them. They got pretty banged up and I'm not sure they're going to be able to get down. Anyway, they're all still alive and stuff, and we told them we'd let you know on our way down and that was only, like, probably four hours ago or so."

I pushed one arm out of the sleeping bag and picked up my tea. Might as well enjoy the rest of it. "So, were they moving when you left, or were they going to stay where they were?"

"Don't know," he said. "We've got to keep going down, gotta

get to the bar down there in Paradise before it closes. Celebrate our summit."

"Just one more thing," I said. "Was anyone going to help them, or were you guys the only ones who were left up there?"

I didn't bother with radio traffic. A visitor had reported an erratic driver near Sunrise Campground, and I could tell that it was going to be a huge incident: several law enforcement rangers were responding and the radio traffic was intense and strained. I got out the cell phone. Charlie was gone for another three weeks climbing in the Bugaboos, and Tom lived in the basement of the visitor center and didn't have a phone. I called the dorm. After I'd let the phone ring a long time, Adrienne answered.

"Hey," I said. "I just heard that some guys got winged by a falling serac right above Ingraham Flats. I'm going to go up and see what I can do for them. If you wouldn't mind, could you call Stefan and ask him if one of the volunteers would be available if this turns into a real emergency and I need help getting these guys down? Just let him know, y'know, I'm going to go up there."

I didn't really know what I wanted to say. Adrienne agreed, though she didn't sound happy, and I gathered that Stefan had been grumpy the last time I'd asked her to talk to him. I told her I'd call her back in ten minutes to see what the news was.

I looked around. It would be dark soon. It was still cold but crisp, and visibility was good. A light cover of hail over the dirty snow made everything look cleaner and more beautiful. The air smelled good. A slight breeze from the southwest kept the smell of the outhouses wafting away from camp, always a sign things were going right. Literally.

I stood on top of the tallest storage box outside the hut and looked up at the mountain through binoculars. I couldn't see anybody on the skyline between Muir and Cathedral Gap. That was most of the way to Ingraham Flats. They really must not be moving. I called Adrienne back.

"Sorry," she said. "Stefan said no, and wanted me to let you know not to call unless you've got a true emergency 'cause we don't have the money for this. Though," she added, "if you really do need help, give me a call and I'll come up and help you."

"Thanks, Adrienne," I said, "I'll let you know." It was sweet of her to offer, but she'd tripped a few days ago and reiunjured her torn anterior cruciate ligament. I knew she could barely walk on it.

I set out alone. A few weak rays of sunshine were barely making it over the edge of the mountain. The sun was disappearing behind this huge shadow, this mountain that blocks out the sky. I was irritated, and feeling angry again. My toes were cold already, or maybe they had never warmed up. My flimsy crampons looked silly on my running shoes, and my heels were starting to wear thin where the straps on the crampons rubbed. I should have put some duct tape on them. I felt embarrassed in my getup. Embarrassed for being alone. Part of my job was to make sure that climbers understood the importance of good gear and safety practices, but I was no example.

I buttoned my town coat and brushed off the sleeves. I reasoned, George Mallory climbed Everest in a tailored cotton jacket . . . oh, but wait, he did die on the descent, or maybe it was on the way up. It would have been nice to rope up, too. Some of the crevasses were large enough that it took a long jump and light thoughts to cross them. With partners, if you fall in you can get hauled back out, feeling warm and fuzzy because your friends are there to save you. I would just have to be careful.

My pack was heavy. I'd taken the first-aid kit, a short rope, and the damp sleeping bag, just in case someone needed it. I also had my compass, a headlamp, a quart of water, and some almond Hershey's bars. I started up Cathedral Gap. It was all rock and steep sand that was exhausting to climb; I slid down with every step. Sometimes on the Gap whole sections would slide, like a rock version of a slab avalanche, with the mud at the top breaking away and leaving a fracture line. It was a scary thing to be on when that happened. Once I'd been helping a group down through this section when it started moving under us, and together we'd all run as fast as we could, knee deep in sand, before it could slide us over the edge and back down to the glacier.

I picked my steps carefully and made it to the top, turning to look back at camp and the pink sky. At the top of the Gap the route turned a corner and started up a little ridge to get to Ingraham Flats. All along the side of this ridge are loose rocks glued together with ice. My crampon's plastic straps hurt my bare ankles whenever the terrain started sloping to the side. It was painful walking, but not that bad, and I felt a bit wussy.

It's fine, I kept telling myself, it's fine, it's fine, it's fine. But I knew the truth: I wasn't. During the off-season my co-workers went to China or Pakistan or Tibet and climbed much harder routes, loving every minute of it. They thrived on near-death experiences, climbing with people they barely knew. All I wanted to do in the off-season was take three or four hot showers a day, cook up huge meals of fresh vegetables, and spend time with friends.

I was pretty sure I still loved the mountains, but I wanted fellowship in the mountains, not judgment or neglect. I didn't want to keep proving myself over and over, when nothing I did seemed to be enough. Climbing alone wore me out and felt like a pointless risk. I wanted more than the act of climbing. I wanted to forge friendships by climbing. I was mad at myself for risking death every day without even that possible payoff. Every adventure I went on alone seemed like a lost opportunity, and constantly climbing alone made my suffering seem meaningless.

I shook my head. The mountain was watching. I wondered

what it thought. I wondered if the mountain felt cold. Wished it could trade places with Ayers Rock in Australia for a few months of glowing red in the sun. Or if it was sad it wasn't a big impressive mountain like K2 with a reputation for killing as many people as it let summit. Hmm. I wondered for an instant what all those people thought about, the second before they died. I'd already planned my last thought. I'd decided there were too many people who died yelling, "Shit!" I wanted to die thinking about white-chocolate-chip macadamia nut cookies. Dying while thinking about dessert seemed unique and tasty and important to me. And I hoped I wouldn't die alone.

The route dropped down a bit going into the flats, and I could see the guys I was looking for, coming towards me. There were three of them, obviously disabled. One was carrying all three packs, and the other two were walking really, really slowly. They were walking, though. I was happy. Mobile was good.

"Hi," I said to the guy in the front of the rope, "I'm Bree, I'm the ranger on duty up here today. Somebody said you got hit by icefall. Are you doing OK?" I squinted at the guy, looking him over for injuries.

"You're the ranger?" He looked me up and down.

"Yes," I said, straightening my nightclub-worthy jacket. "I'm here to help you. Would you like a Hershey's almond chocolate bar?" The man with the three packs was Native American. He looked old, maybe in his sixties, and he wore his waist-long hair in two braids down his back. He was wearing an ancient green plaid wool jacket that buttoned in the front, and had a huge digital camera slung over one shoulder.

"I'd love a chocolate bar," he said, and then added, "I'm OK walking for now, but the guys are pretty tired. We did get hit by the ice. One of the guys broke his collarbone, and maybe some ribs, and he got kind of cut up when he got hit with a chunk of ice. The other guy had a bad knee, so of course that's the one he fell over on when he dove out of the way."

"But you're fine? Are you doing OK carrying all the packs?"

"Yeah, but we've got a lot of stuff down at Camp Muir and I'm not going to be able to carry all of that."

"We'll worry about that when we get down there. You guys seem to be doing just fine. Did you hang out where you got hit for a while, or have you been trying to descend since the accident?" I was going to be very worried if they'd been moving the whole time, because they'd made it less than five hundred feet in several hours.

"We stopped for a long time," he said. "We were tuckered out, anyways. We left camp to start climbing twenty-one hours ago." I was relieved, and walked over to the other two.

The second guy on the rope had a bad case of acne. He looked young, maybe about eighteen, with a bloody bandana wrapped around his head. "Are you the bad knee guy, or the guy who got hit by the icefall?" I asked, to make conversation.

"Icefall," he answered, humorlessly.

"Your friend says you might have broken your collarbone and some ribs. I've got a first-aid kit, want me to see what I can do to help?" I unzipped his jackets and lifted up his shirt. There was a huge black bruise the size of a basketball on the side of his chest.

"You having any trouble breathing?" I asked.

"Hurts, but I can do it."

"Sweet."

"Cold though."

"OK." I rezipped his jackets. It's a fantastic thing about the mountain: By the time I get to people they're often either fine, or already dead. It saves a lot of work trying to figure out what's a critical injury and what isn't.

"I can give you a sling for your arm, and it should make your collarbone feel better," I said.

"Do you have to take my jacket off again?"

"Nope."

"Sweet."

I dug out the first-aid kit and came up with a couple of triangle bandages, which I used to tie a sling and swath. "Nothing else hurt?"

"Nope."

"Sweet."

I handed him a chocolate bar and walked on to the third guy. "Knee guy?" He looked up. He kind of looked like a hippie, I guessed in his thirties, with a big black beard. He had two ice axes, which I noticed he'd been using as really short crutches before his party had sat down for their break.

"Is there anything I can do to help, or can you keep walking out on it as-is?" I wasn't going to give him any options where he didn't have to walk out, because today, he didn't have any.

"It's fine," he replied.

"I'll give you my trekking poles," I said. "That'll be a lot easier than the ice axes."

I walked back to the first guy, and said, "Let's get our headlamps out now, and then we won't have to stop again later."

We started back to camp. I was afraid they weren't going to make it up the tiny uphill right before the start of the ridge, but we did a rest step: Take a step. Count to four. Take another step.

It was full dark before we even got to the top of Cathedral Gap. There wasn't any moon and the stars were really bright. It had finished clearing, and there wasn't a cloud in sight. The hippie guy knew all the constellations, and when we took breaks he'd show them to the rest of us. I said that sometimes in the early morning you could see a little bit of the northern lights, just a bit of a green wave before dawn. There wasn't anything there yet tonight. We all agreed that was too bad.

My light made a circle on the snow in front of me. I couldn't see anything outside of it, and felt claustrophobic to be stuck inside it, dependent on it to get me down. I resolved to stop thinking about it, and then after a while I stopped thinking about anything. Somebody would stumble or groan, and I'd say, "You all right?" But we all just had to keep walking.

When we got to Muir, I asked, "What do you want to do?"

"We want to keep going, he needs to go to the hospital," said the Native American, pointing at the acne kid.

"That's true, he probably does," I said, and resigned myself to this trip taking longer than I'd planned. They didn't really need me to go with them—if they left all their stuff at Muir, if everything worked out perfectly for them, if they didn't get lost in the dark with the unfamiliar ice, if the guy's crushed chest held up as it had been. And if they stayed here? Maybe the kid would die in his sleep. They looked at me expectantly. "OK" I said. "I'll help you guys down. Where's your tent?"

I packed up their stuff and wondered why people carry so much crap up to Muir. There was no way they'd used this many spare pairs of long underwear, and what was the point of having a second spare fuel canister? I made up one huge pack and combined the other two into a strange-looking contraption with a bunch of gear sticking out the back and sides, then I struggled into one of the beasts. The force of it hitting my back made me stumble forward a few steps and I regretted not having my trekking poles to steady the load and save my dissolving, creaking knees. Somebody from a nearby tent yelled that some people had to get up and climb in the morning, and could I please be quiet. "Sorry, we'll be gone in a minute," I whispered.

I gave the other pack to the Native American, and we headed down from Muir towards the tiny lights of Paradise. There is nothing to say about the trip except that it was long, and that we made it. I left them in the parking lot with some handwritten directions to Good Samaritan Hospital in Tacoma.

"We didn't even summit," one of them said sadly in the dark.

"It really doesn't matter," I said. "It really doesn't."

In the dorm, the kitchen lights were on. Someone, probably Adrienne, had made blueberry muffins before going to sleep. They were hers, but I ate them anyway. I was only going to eat one muffin, but once I'd eaten one I couldn't stop, and I ended up eating most of the dozen. They were fantastic. Then I decided I fancied some Eggos, and I pulled out another eight. "Tonight, I will eat them with jam," I thought, and filled up each one of the little square indents in the top with raspberry jam. Tasty and pretty. I inhaled them.

I took off my wet running shoes. They were showing a lot of wear from the crampons, with holes on both sides of the toes from the front bail. My feet weren't doing much better, and neither was my out-on-the-town coat for that matter. I was too tired to take a shower, so I set my alarm and went to bed still wearing all my clothes. Every joint and muscle in my body ached, and it was only day two of my eight-day shift. Before falling asleep, I wondered briefly if I should add an iron supplement to my diet.

Alarm. Six in the morning. Dizzy, I stood up and clutched at the bedpost. It was going to be a sunny day, maybe even warm. I squatted down to get my shoes off the boot drier, but then my knees refused to let me stand up again and I ended up having to sit down, roll over, and awkwardly push myself back up. Damn people with their damn heavy packs. I spent a little while looking for my pack before I realized I'd left it up at Muir. I didn't really need to bring anything with me anyway, it was all up there already. I put my Park Service radio in one pocket and my keys in the other, slung my crampons over my shoulder, went to the kitchen, and drank a quart of orange Gatorade without coming up for air.

Then I grabbed a handful of store-bought gingersnap cookies for breakfast, and headed out.

I was tired and it took a long time to get to Muir. It was almost warm when I got there. I'd taken my on-the-town jacket off and wrapped it around my waist, going for the professional uniform jacket look. Nobody was around to notice.

My feet really needed some duct tape. I rummaged around at Muir for some, and then pulled my shoes off and wrung my socks out. My heels were bleeding, and my toes weren't doing a whole lot better. I covered everything with duct tape—big strips across each heel, and short pieces for each one of my toes, individually wrapped. Much better, if a little weird-looking. I put my socks back on. Yes, better.

Rich called on the radio to say he was headed up to Camp Muir and needed help fixing some stuff with the outhouses. I liked Rich, but I had been hoping for a day focused more on visitor contacts and less on heavy lifting. I sat and pouted for a few minutes, staring out through the door of the hut at Muir Rock across the way, where a few people were practicing ice-ax arrest. I sucked it up. I needed to clean up the hut.

I started putting my food away and turned the tiny stove back on to try to melt the pot of ice again. Last night had pretty much undone any progress I'd made melting it. I needed to clean my soup pot out from yesterday, too, I remembered. It was still sitting outside the front door—with tomato residue dried onto the bottom and a layer of sand that had blown in and fused to the tomato. It was going to be a hard job, and it was going to have to wait for hot water. I pulled my damp sleeping bag out of my pack, turned it inside out, and hung it out to dry over one of the giant cables that kept the hut grounded in high winds.

The guide service was still out climbing, I noticed. They took a new group of clients up almost every night. Usually one or two clients wouldn't leave Camp Muir because they were out of shape, or didn't feel well, and then one or two more would turn around with a guide somewhere on the route because they were out of shape, or didn't feel well, and the rest would summit and return around noon. Today I noticed that one of the clients who had stayed at camp was having a yelling match with one of the guides. I closed the door and continued putting my cans of food back into my bin.

A minute later, there was a knock on the door. It was the guide. He looked pissed. He squeezed in and shut the door. It was a small hut for two people. If we'd been sitting opposite each other our knees would have touched. "Want some tea?" I asked. "I'll have some water up here in a bit," I added, waving at the tiny stove and the big pot on the countertop.

The guide's eyes narrowed as he viewed the setup. "Bigger problems, Bree. Bigger problems. I've got this super irritating client, *Richard*." The name came out like a growl. "He wants to go down. Says he doesn't like us. But we just can't let him go. He's our responsibility. But he was threatening to just take off back down the mountain, so we took away his boots. Now he's super mad and is demanding them back. All the senior guides are still out on the mountain. Will you talk to him?"

"You stole his boots?" I asked, incredulous.

"What were we supposed to do? He has to stay! It's too dangerous for him alone. We can all go down together this afternoon."

"I'd be pissed if you stole my shoes," I said.

"Yeah, but we wouldn't steal your shoes."

"Thanks," I grinned.

"Maybe just give me a moment alone with him," I said. "Have you tried calling your office for direction?"

"We've been trying to get through, I'll go try it again." He left and jogged up the stairs into one of their buildings.

I walked over to the client and held out my hand. "Hi, Richard, I'm Bree, I'm the ranger on duty up here today."

He looked like he was in his early fifties. He had brand-new climbing clothes on, and a little bit of a gut. He was probably a doctor or a lawyer or something, I thought. And he was walking around with just a pair of thick, red-toed, gray wool socks on his feet.

"What's the difference between a ranger and a guide?" he asked. "Besides, you look more like one of the cooks."

"Um," I said, "I work for the government, I'm in charge of the camp up here right now, and although I work with these guides to make sure everything runs smoothly, part of my job is guide service monitoring for quality control. So if you have a concern, you can tell me and I'll make sure it gets addressed."

"I was willing to wait to go down with them this afternoon, until they stole my boots," Richard said grumpily. "I'm an adult, I'm competent, I'm declining their services, they can't keep me prisoner here. Make them give me my boots back."

"OK," I said. "I think the one guy just got a little bit upset. I'll get him to give your boots back. I guess the thing is that it is safer to go down with the guide service if you don't have any experience, and there's some additional gear that it would be nice to have, like a map and compass. I mean, you hired a guide in the first place because you thought you needed one. Maybe it would be better to be patient, work out your personality differences in the parking lot, and then go for a beer?"

He looked at me for a long moment. "Nope."

I went back up to babysit my water pot. It was coming along nicely. Richard and the guide followed me. "The office says we have to give his boots back. He can leave if he really wants to, as long as there's a witness, you, hearing me telling him that it's really dangerous and we're not responsible for him anymore—that if he's seriously injured or dies, it's not our fault and he won't sue us."

"He's right there," I said. "Does that count, or do you have to do it again?"

"Richard," the guide said, turning towards him, "if you refuse our services we can't guarantee your protection and you might, and probably will, fall in a crevasse and die, and it won't be our fault, and you can't sue us. Do you understand?"

"I get it already," Richard said, "you can go now." The guide stalked off back to his own hut, but Richard stayed sitting on the storage box outside. I went back inside to pump the stove up again.

"Um," said Richard, "so the thing is, I don't really feel comfortable going down by myself, but that whole boot-stealing thing was bullshit and I couldn't stand that. So, what are my options to get down from here?"

"Well," I answered, "you could suck it up and go down by yourself since that's the decision you made, or you could go over to the campground where all the independent climbers are, and see if anyone is going down and if they'd be willing to let you tag along."

"When are you headed down?" Richard asked.

"Later today," I said. "I've got a project to work on in Paradise tomorrow, but I've got to wait for the maintenance guy to come up here so I can help him fix some stuff with the outhouses."

"They're disgusting," he said. I let it slide. But I saw my chance of getting out of working on the shitters.

"OK, Richard," I said, "I'll take you down to the top of Panorama Point. But then I have to stop and do some work there, so you'll have to go down the trail yourself, OK?"

"Good," said Richard. "Let's go."

I knew it was going to take the rest of the day to go with Richard, and that was fine with me. I wouldn't have to stay up here late working with Rich. I could stop and clean the bathroom at Pan Point and be back in Paradise around the time I got off the clock. Perfect. I scribbled an apology, tacked it to the door, and closed up the hut.

I could call Richard an "assist" on my accountability form, but this was shaping up to be a grim week for proving my worth to the bureaucracy. Assists didn't matter very much, and there was no space to explain why my assists took such a long time. It was already the end of day three, and I still hadn't checked off anything under the "projects achieved" section. That was the really important section. I hadn't even gotten a summit climb in. My boss would wonder what I was doing with my time.

9

ROADTRIP RESCUE

I HAD JUST POURED THE LAST OF MY MILK on the last of my Honey Nut Cheerios. The sun was baking in the front windows of the Paradise dorm. I picked up my bowl and moved to an armchair that we'd balanced on top of a couple of sheets of plywood, on top of a couple of folding chairs' and cinder blocks. From the chair, I was high enough to see the peaks of the Tatoosh through the kitchen windows. When I climbed up on it, the whole contraption groaned and wobbled, and the cushion support had ripped out of the chair, but it would hold if I eased onto it. I stretched out in this sunny spot, the hot fabric of the dark brocade against my back, and felt my cold stiff body absorb the heat like a dry sponge in water.

I noticed I had terrible tan lines. My leg hair was bleached white—it was too much work to shave anymore—and my legs were tan, but I had a white sock line around my ankles, and then my feet were pure red, white, and blue. I opened the window, stuck my feet out, and let them wave and dry in the sun three storeys above the visitor center parking lot.

The whole evening stretched out before me: First I would eat Cheerios and sleep here until the sun crossed over the Tatoosh and no longer came in the kitchen window; then I would make lasagna and chocolate chip cookies, leaving a few for Tom and Charlie, who were bouldering down in Longmire; and then I would go to bed around seven-thirty. I would creak down onto the bed, savoring the pain of the change in position, the backache that made it hard to breathe at first, but then I would conform to the mattress completely, embrace it, pull the covers over my head, and shut everything out. The evening would be fantastic.

I closed my eyes and made an invisible soundproof line above all the traffic and honking in the parking lot, the people crowding the trails, the screaming children in the visitor center, the constant party hosted by the Paradise Inn and restaurant employees going on behind us in the next housing block over. Done with the mountain for the day, I felt a semblance of peace. And then there was the sound of feet pounding up the stairs.

"Are you going?" asked Tom as he stumbled, giggling, into the kitchen, his climbing shoes in one hand. "Do you have any food I can eat?"

As a volunteer, Tom didn't get paid, but otherwise we all had the same job. I tried to feed him when I could. He was tall, with big feet and greasy dark hair. He came from Corvallis, Oregon, and I thought his parents were farmers, but he had occasional moments of confusion when he thought he was a gangster rapper from New York. The previous summer, we'd stayed together in Seattle for a few days for a firefighting class, and we'd gone to Broadway on Capitol Hill. He'd made me drive the street again and again so he could look at all the crazy people with big hair, talking to themselves and waving at things that weren't there. Like he'd never seen crazy people before.

Now I looked over at him and saw his pink fleecy hat perched at an incredible angle on top of his greasy head. Today's signature piece: He was a crazy person. He opened the refrigerator.

"I thought you guys already went climbing?" I murmured with my eyes closed. I didn't want to go climbing, I wanted to stay here and sleep. I didn't want to spend my super-rare free evening in a broken-down barn in Longmire clinging to greasy plastic holds attached to a rotting piece of plywood. I wasn't sure how they could spend so much time there. I started to panic about being forced to go.

"No," he said impatiently, "not that." He closed the refrigerator door and straightened up. "We've been officially requested by the Ashford Fire Department to rescue some hiker in the hills above town." He grinned broadly, and I stared at him.

"I thought they had a volunteer fire department to do that stuff, and what about the guide service who are actually based in the town. Can't they do it?" I asked.

"I don't know," Tom said. "I suppose we have some sort of reciprocity agreement with them. Maybe we used them for something in the past."

He opened the refrigerator again. I knew I had to suggest some food I didn't mind losing, or he'd move on to my cabinet and start eating my chocolate bars. "I think there's some cheese and tortillas in there, you could make some quesadillas. I think Charlie has some salsa, you could use his."

"Sweet, Bree's making quesadillas?" said Charlie, turning the corner from the stairs down the hallway to his room.

"No!" I yelled after him down the hall, "you can use my cheese and tortillas, but you're making them, and make me one, too."

"Who's organizing this rescue?" I asked Tom.

"Uh, I think Tim is, and he requested six people. He might have them by now, and come to think of it, he doesn't like you, you probably shouldn't call him at all. Just come down with us and we'll all go together. You might not get paid, if they already have enough people, but it's better than just sitting around here." Tom looked around at the silent kitchen and the dust floating in the sun. His nose wrinkled. "This is frickin' boring."

I liked just sitting. I could easily do it all day without experiencing even a twinge of boredom. But if everybody else was out doing something together and I wasn't, my napping plans would be ruined. Instead I'd mope about missing the social interaction and, well, maybe they really needed more people. It takes a lot of people to carry a person. People are heavy. I sighed and got up. "What do I need to bring, Tom?"

"Nothing, I don't think. I mean, it's just in the woods, right?"

"Cool," I said. "That sounds perfect."

It was a warm summer day, and all of a sudden I was actually looking forward to a hike in the woods, where there wasn't any snow, and where none of my stuff would get wet, and it wouldn't be freezing cold, and if I accidentally slipped I wouldn't fall to my death in a crevasse. It had been a long time since I'd walked on a sunny trail in the woods, surrounded by new growth and huge old trees, with the springy ground under my feet. It was good on the knees, I remembered. I went to my room and picked up my backpack, putting a quart of water in it along with a jacket, headlamp, and chocolate bar.

"Hey, Charlie," I yelled down the hall. "Uniforms?" It was up to Charlie to make these kinds of complicated calls.

"I'm not wearing mine," he yelled back through his closed door. That was good, I only owned one, and at the moment it reeked.

We piled into the blue government minivan, with quesadillas and the rest of my sodas in hand. We maneuvered out of the parking lot—oblivious to traffic and scenery alike—around the gawking tourists in the road and past the tailgate picnickers, their dinners complete with chips and cheap Rainier beer.

Charlie turned on the Funky Monkey, his favorite radio station, and cranked up the volume. He was always threatening to call the station from Camp Muir, say who we were, and then add that we were their highest listeners. It was that sort of station. Tom had been in Las Vegas the week before, getting paid for working as a wild-land firefighter, and he'd picked up dozens of call-girl cards, amazed at the novelty of the idea. Every time we took a corner, the cards slid back and forth on the van's floor. I was going to have to clean those out before anyone borrowed our government van, along with the rearview mirror ornament, a magazine cutout of George Bush sporting a three-millimeter-cord noose. Not that I objected to it on principle.

There was a lot of traffic on the road. We slowed to a crawl behind an RV, the owner with his head actually out the window, both hands too, shading the viewfinder on the obligatory oversized digital camera. We cursed him like we were doing something important and it was vital we got to our destination in a hurry. Sometimes if you generate enough excitement, you don't need anything substantial to back it up, the momentum alone is enough. Windows down and music cranked, we continued following the RV.

We finally got to Longmire after forty minutes on a road that usually takes less than thirty, and met up with Tim. He was in full uniform, including his bulletproof vest and gun belt with thirty pounds of odd gadgets Velcroed to it. I suppose he was obligated to wear the uniform, but I could tell he liked it—it was in his swagger, the way he hooked his thumbs in his belt and stuck out his pelvis, as if to show off all his equipment. He scowled at me when I got out of the minivan, but we didn't say anything to each other and I figured he must still be short of people for the carryout. He knew that I knew I wouldn't get paid for this outing unless I went over to talk to him, but he didn't know that I knew it wasn't worth the money.

We caravanned, fast, bumper-to-bumper, down the road from Longmire and out of the park, passing under the giant log hoisted above the roadway with the wooden park sign dangling below it— all of that awesome, rotting tonnage looming over the cars, trucks, and vans lined up to pay at the toll booth. Tim was in the lead with his marked patrol SUV. We were next in the blue, dirty, and over-loaded minivan. Then behind us was a backcountry ranger I hadn't met before in a dusty, rusty Subaru wagon.

I've always loved caravans. They're absurd. Only the first driver is given any information about where everyone is going, forcing the rest of the line to disobey traffic signals, brush off merging traf-fic, and follow too close in order to keep the leader in sight. One time when I was sixteen, driving (with only a learner's permit) in a bumper-to-bumper caravan to a youth-based rescue group out-ing, I created a chain-reaction pileup totaling three vehicles when I accidentally hit the clutch instead of the brake. Even so, I still love the common purpose of a caravan, the obvious signals we give other drivers to show we're together, and the feeling that the destination is important because all the other people you're with want to go there, too.

We turned off onto a logging road in Ashford after picking up another ranger who had been waiting to rendezvous with us. It was much warmer in Ashford than it had been thousands of feet higher in Paradise. It felt good to be in the minivan with the sun beating down and the windows rolled up, air vents blowing road dirt on us, coating everything with a layer of dust. It smelled like summer and the earth and the solid, inviting woods.

As we headed into the hills outside of Ashford the road got worse, narrow and tilted, filled with water traps and humps and valleys. We turned from one unmarked junction to another until we were sure we were lost. Charlie was clinging to the steering wheel with both hands and peering out through two layers of dust trying to follow Tim's SUV. Charlie was grinning madly. He turned on the wipers, and that helped the dust a little, but the sun was low enough to shine right in our eyes. Tom and I just held on, happy for every inch of this road that could be driven instead of walked, content with being bounced along towards whatever end.

After nearly an hour on dirt logging roads, we finally hit a dead end, a tiny turnaround filled with dusty, dry potholes, surrounded on one side by woods and on the other by an overgrown clearcut. The turnaround was occupied by the victim's truck and the Ashford Fire Department's dusty, aged aid car. When we arrived, the driver's door of the aid car opened and an ancient man stepped out. He must have been at least ninety, wearing a hand-knit wool sweater despite the heat, Velcro fire department patches on the arms. He pulled his cane from behind the seat, donned his white helmet, and fastened the chin strap with shaking fingers. He was unsteady walking across the lot, and Charlie leapt out of the minivan and offered his elbow. Through the passenger's window I could see an old woman, presumably the Fire Chief's wife, happily knitting in the front seat. I began to understand why they had called the Park Service.

The old Chief was definitely in charge, though. I had nothing but respect for him as he ordered us all around, including Tim, telling us what gear to take and what the plan was (hike in, pick up the injured hiker, and hike out). I could tell Tim was upset that he wasn't even allowed to have a huddle meeting first, before being relegated to working with the lot of us scruffy, backcountry folk.

One of the members of the volunteer fire department was already with the victim, who was a man in his forties who'd turned an ankle on the trail and couldn't walk the last mile to the road. That sounded fine to me. The whole carryout should be fast and stress-free. The five of us from the park threw on our packs, grabbed the equipment we would need, and started up the trail a few minutes later, leaving the Fire Chief and his wife to watch over base camp.

The woods were as fantastic as I'd thought they would be. The late-afternoon sun slid between the trees and onto the trail, onto us. The trail itself was a mass of old, knotted roots from the huge, equally gnarled trees still standing guard on the edge of the clearcut above town. Along the trail were blueberry bushes, right at eye level. After a few minutes of hiking and looking at the fat, untouched blueberries, we couldn't stay away from them any longer. We knew this fellow with a sprained ankle would be fine for a few more minutes, and as a perennially hungry group we put down our packs and wandered into the woods for a "water break," eating and stuffing our pockets and hats with berries. The backcountry rangers were used to foraging all the time, but for Charlie, Tom, and me, who always worked in the snow, it was as sweet as it gets. We left Tim on the trail to start evaluating the terrain for the carryout.

Once we started back up the trail, wiping blue fingers on our shorts, we got to the victim in no time. He was probably only a half-mile from the turnaround, lying on the warm dirt and pine needles with his injured leg stuck out in front of him, already splinted, and attended by the sixth man, a slightly younger volunteer firefighter who used to work for the Park Service. He was probably the one who had suggested calling us.

We got to them just as the sun was going behind the hills and we were down to the flat light of dusk, but it was still a warm, summer dusk, complete with mosquitoes, pests I hadn't seen for a while. I didn't mind them, it was nice to see animal life again, even if they were blood-sucking insects. They made the summer feel real, genuine, complete with all the important details and variety that were lacking in the mountain's austere snow and ice and rock.

"Do you need to pee?" I asked the man. Everybody looked at me. I realized this was a lame way to introduce myself, so I followed with, "It'll take us a little time to get back to the cars, so if you have to pee, pee now." OK, I was done talking.

We got the victim to lie down in the old one-piece metal litter. Then we picked him up about four feet in the air and attached the litter's huge, knobby wheel to the bottom of it. That way, if we all held on to both sides we could wheel him out without actually carrying his entire weight, which just from picking him up I realized was considerable.

Tim immediately took charge. He put two people on each side of the litter, which was tipping wildly on its central dirt-bike wheel, and then he put one person on each end to help brake the contraption as we negotiated the steep downhill sections over knee-high drop-offs (courtesy of the root systems) and big rocks in the trail. I'm not sure how many litter evacuations Tim had done in his long career, or where they might have occurred or in what kind of terrain, but his directions weren't going over well on this one. The trails in Paradise, where most of our carryouts happen, are wide, only slightly sloping, and mostly paved.

As we grunted our way down the trail here, Tim, the man in the front, was walking backwards. He kept tripping over things behind him that he couldn't see. The rest of us, crowded together, kept stepping on each other's feet, and we couldn't see where we were going, either. Every time Tim tripped, he got angry with us for going too fast, or not fast enough, over an obstacle we didn't know was there.

I should have kept my mouth shut, but I just couldn't. I am chronically bad at keeping quiet when there's a simple solution to an obvious problem. For ten years I'd been a member of a youth-based lowland search and rescue group that I was embarrassed to tell anyone about, because now as a professional I wasn't supposed to fraternize with amateurs. But I had done hundreds of carryouts through the woods, and I had a few ideas about how to make this one better. I figured that Tim didn't like me anyway, so what the hell? I opened my mouth.

"Hey, guys," I said, "hold up a minute."

"Are you tired?" Tim mocked, looking at his watch without letting go of the litter, and then he snapped, "You have another seven

minutes." One of his other favorite evacuation methods was allow-
ing us only prescheduled breaks. I can't stand regimentation when
it's totally unnecessary. Maybe if we were a huge group of people
it would make sense, but with just six of us we could afford to be
more flexible. I stewed about this for a second before realizing that
we were still stopped and everybody was still looking at me.

"Let's switch around," I said, leaning the litter against my
thigh. "My left arm is definitely longer now than my right one."
I held up both my arms, with one shoulder back so that my fingertips on the hand grasping the litter were a good six inches past
my other hand. Since girls are the weaker sex, I decided I might as
well use that, and a little humor, to my advantage. Tom chuckled
in the dark, and I thanked him silently.

I had pulled a ten-foot piece of one-inch tubular webbing out
of the van because I'd thought it might be useful, and now I got it
out of my pack. I tied it to the rear of the litter, walked out five feet,
and tied a loop in it for a handle. I had Charlie, a Greek statue of a
man, hold onto the end as the brake, where he was far enough out
of the way that we wouldn't be stepping on each other. Since Tim
was doing no good in the front, I asked him to take up my position
on the side, and while I'm sure he glared at me, it was nearly dark
and I couldn't see it. I also figured that, since this reorganization
stemmed from my perceived weakness, it would mitigate his dis-
sent. It worked; he went along with it.

I felt bad for a minute because Charlie was my boss, and I didn't
want to step on his toes. I would follow any sort of order he could
come up with, but he didn't seem interested in dealing with Tim. I
understood that. They worked together more often than Tim and I
did, and I supposed that Charlie needed to save what power he had
for vetoing Tim when it was a matter of life and death. I figured I
wouldn't offend Charlie too badly by taking over this short carryout. It was a me-sized rescue.

I didn't like the big rescues anymore, the ones with helicopters flying overhead, the media storming Longmire, and people screaming and bleeding in the snow after a few unspeakable moments of terror. I'd discovered that these operations were too complicated for anyone to keep them in check; they had a life of their own. They were impersonal and stressful and left me feeling like I had no control over my own destiny—so much energy, money, and power were spent to do the rescue, and getting good media coverage was so important that it seemed to me as if it didn't matter what or who was sacrificed in the attempt as long as the rescue was successful. Like it was more important for everybody to come off looking heroic for the sake of the climbing program and its future budget than for everyone to come back in one piece. I could handle my small part in the big rescue, but the following nights found me looking back and analyzing what I'd done, which so closely mirrored what the victims had done—often we'd both been in the same spot, dodged the same rocks, jumped the same crevasse, only now one of us was severely injured or dead. Even if the press conference went well, and the whole thing was deemed a success, it left me feeling like death was looming over my shoulder.

This basic carryout might just have been my favorite day of the season. A day with a simple story and a happy ending.

We started off again with just four people actually touching the litter. Everyone was able to see what was ahead without crowding each other's feet. Charlie and his enormous muscles were providing more than enough braking power, and I walked out about ten feet in front and called out obstacles on the trail, where they were, how big they were, and which side they were on. The carryout was going more smoothly, but whether that would make up for the widening rift between Tim and me, I had no idea. I figured it didn't matter at that point, so I also changed the rules: any time someone wanted a break, we stopped.

In actuality, it wasn't far back to the road, though it was nearly full dark when we got there. The old Fire Chief had the ambulance's scene lights on, and hundreds of moths were flying around them, offering up flicking noises as their wings brushed against the lights. Tim was back in charge. I held the side of the litter while the wheel was removed, and then we set the whole thing on the ground and let the poor guy back out. He opted to drive home himself with his good foot. Tim and the Fire Chief had a few words—they finally had their huddle—and they shook hands, some obligation fulfilled.

Tim walked over to where we were all sitting in the minivan. "Bree," he addressed my silhouette with his own outline holding a clipboard, "you didn't really help very much."

I blushed in the dark. I was pretty sure I had expedited the actual rescue, but I also had to admit it did seem lazy just walking ahead of the litter. Sometimes a gesture of mindless physical involvement, a willingness to suffer with others, goes a long way towards creating trust and friendship. "But I'll put your name down on the overtime list."

"Thanks, Tim," I said, surprised by his generosity and, more than anything, that he had actually come to me. Maybe there was hope. I stammered, "I really appreciate it. I'll do better next time, I promise." He swiveled and walked away, hoisted himself back into his SUV, and took off.

Tom drove us back down the road after the ambulance, bumping slowly along in the dark. As the last car down we couldn't see anything through the dust, and Tom was driving amazingly close to the ambulance's back bumper. It was exciting, like we were cars on a roller coaster: we'd see the tail lights in front of us suddenly disappear into a giant hole, and we'd brace ourselves for the inevitable crunch and scrape of our frame as we were drawn inexorably forward. We'd see the lights suddenly rise above us to the level of the top of our windshield, and Tom would gun it for all it was worth, and our bald little wheels would spin mercilessly against the loose dust of the rise. I liked it. Tom smiled, hunched over the wheel. No one said anything, we just watched the lights and the darkness.

When we made it back to Ashford we decided to go out for pie before heading back. Technically, we were on call even though the paid workday had ended, and we should have hightailed it back to the park. But Charlie said if anyone turned out to have been looking for us, we'd just say we'd had a flat tire on the dirt road, which was pretty plausible. Charlie was too honest, his conscience usually sent him straight home, but today if he wanted to stop for pie, we were only going to support him.

Blinking in the sudden light, I teetered in the roadside restaurant outside the park entrance, my joints stiff again. I was pleasantly surprised that the place was still open. I had been up climbing since the previous midnight, and I'd lost track of time, not sure how late it was. The little café seemed so homey and bright inside, there were so many colors—it was dazzlingly, amazingly beautiful. I fingered the plastic red-and-white checkered tablecloth, and ordered two slices of the most delicious blackberry pie.

10

POINT OF NO RETURN

THE SUMMER WAS OVER. It was eight o'clock in the morning on my last day. My final responsibility was winterizing the Climbing Information Center. I'd just finished cleaning out the recycling bin and mopping the newly refurbished soft pine floor. As if cleaning it would erase the damage done by hundreds of boots owned by hundreds of climbers who had nervously ground loose gravel into the finish while waiting for me to issue them a permit. The floor was hopeless, but doling out permits had been fun for me. "We are already very full," I'd say, shaking my head at my computer, and then barely manage to squeeze the party in. It always made them feel lucky. I think it's important to feel lucky when you climb.

My boss, Stefan, was in the back office cleaning up loose ends of his own. I could see him watching me though the window every time I turned around, making sure I was still working, or maybe he was just reassured to know someone else was there. The CIC was already closed for the season, and we were the only rangers left in Paradise. The cavernous space was so quiet it seemed oppressive. I set the mop abruptly down against the counter, and it slid off and slammed to the floor, the noise like a shot. I jumped, even though I'd watched it fall. I had to get out of the building, so

I skipped to the next thing on my to-do list: switching over to the self-registration system. I left the mop, figuring there was no one left to trip over it.

I'd already written up directions for using the climbers' self-registration system, and all I had left to do was to put the directions on the box outside. The box was there because there wasn't a high enough volume of climbers to justify keeping the CIC open over the winter, but there were still people who wanted to climb the mountain in the off-season. So to keep track of them in case they went missing, the park let them self-register.

I walked into the back office to look for a screwdriver so I could put the self-registration directions underneath the Plexiglas plate on top of the box. We had bags of miscellaneous tools, boxes of rusted-out wrenches, and thousands of zip-ties, but although I found six large flathead screwdrivers, there weren't any Phillips. I thought briefly about trying to use a flathead, but I remembered that I had nearly stripped the screws last year by using an oversized flathead for this same project. Stefan was making phone calls, and I could tell that my banging around in the back was starting to bother him, so I decided to walk over to the Paradise Inn to borrow the right tool.

Outside it was a beautiful fall morning. The meadows were dead, but the stalks which had so recently flowered were now covered with frosty cobwebs that sparkled in the sunshine. The air was cold and clean, so healthy it was painful. The sidewalk, still icy, crunched a little bit under my boots where the sun hadn't hit it yet. Even so, I could tell it was going to warm up fast enough that I'd be comfortable without a jacket by mid-afternoon. It was a perfect day, I thought to myself, a lucky day, my last day.

I remembered I had a finishing hammer and a few other tools in the trunk of my car. I wasn't sure where the tools had come from originally, and they'd been banging around in my trunk for so long I was thinking of taking them out, but I thought this might just be the project that would earn them their keep for another few years. My car was in the main parking lot, sort of on the way to the Inn, and I walked slowly out there first, enjoying the sunshine and the fact that Stefan wasn't watching me as I wove through the few frost-covered cars in the lot. Sure enough, I had the right screwdriver. It had a blue handle, and looked like it had never been used before. I stuck it in my pocket and headed back to the self-registration box.

I got two of the screws out by just pulling up on the plastic top. They were little, rusted, stripped screws, and I was deeply satisfied with myself for getting them out so fast. I even thought briefly about trying to find new, bigger screws to replace the old ones with—a job truly beyond the call of duty for my last day— when I overheard the garbageman calling the communications center over my radio. A car with four people in it had driven off the road and gone over Christine Falls. The garbageman was deaf and his speech was a little garbled, so although he had a radio and could transmit, nobody could call him back to ask questions. The communications center immediately started calling Stefan, but he didn't answer. I figured he was probably still on the phone.

I could feel my heart start to beat faster, but I didn't know if I'd heard what I thought I'd heard and, anyway, I didn't know if Stefan would want me to go. Above all, I didn't want anything to come between me and the exit lane at the park entrance. I needed to be cruising under the cedar log arch at four-thirty sharp, be-cause I had a date with peace. Part of me longed for the winter season and its safe, normal routine after difficult months of work, a reprieve from a lifestyle I was beginning to suspect was causing me post-traumatic stress disorder.

And yet I found myself gearing up for one last rescue. Some part of me knew this would be the last time I would put myself out there, and I wanted to do it right. I didn't know then that Charlie would die in an avalanche a few months later—days after

announcing his engagement and plans to go to nursing school—
or that Mike would opt for a totally fresh team by replacing me
as well as my dead friend. He would tell me then that he thought
I wasn't mentally prepared to give the job everything, in light of
Charlie's accident, and it was true. But before that happened, on
the last day of my third season, some part of me already knew that
I was about to be done. I wanted to live a long and happy life. I
wanted to climb for fun, with friends; get married and buy a house
in the country; own lawn chairs, have babies, grow organic peas. I
wanted to save myself next. It was one thing to live for climbing,
it was another to know it was only a matter of time before you
died for it.

I stuffed the self-registration papers and the screwdriver back
in my pocket and jammed the screws back in their holes just as the
communications center called me, looking for Stefan. I ran faster
than was strictly necessary back to the CIC and motioned to Stefan to get off the phone. He waved me off and so I waited, spinning
the mop behind the counter with impatience, until he was done
with his conversation.

When I told him what I'd heard, he said he didn't think a car
could go over Christine Falls because there was a three-foot-high,
three-foot-thick concrete barrier, covered with decorative river
rock, constructed just to prevent cars from driving over the falls.
He told me to take the Paradise ambulance down to the falls and
find out what the real problem was. If there actually was a car
down the embankment, he said, I should call him on the radio,
and he'd bring down the rope-rescue equipment so we could pull
everybody back up again. I could tell he didn't want his day complicated, either. It was warm in the back office where the sun came
in, and he had the only comfortable chair in the place.

I ran out the main entrance and across the parking lot. I liked
being looked at by the few tourists bumming around, the lone

uniformed ranger running at top speed with her radio in hand, obviously a vital part of the solution of some horrible catastrophe. I often did this for fun early in the season, even when there was no emergency, just to see the reactions I got.

I started down the road the eighth of a mile to where the ambulance was parked just outside my dorm. I wanted to stop in at the dorm to grab some breakfast before I started down the hill, so I had to hurry. I was thinking that this could be a long last day.

The Paradise maintenance guy, Guy, drove up alongside me, matching my pace, and rolled down his window to offer me a ride. I jumped in. His little red truck smelled like old cigarette smoke. Guy was excited to be part of the action. Just the previous week he had gotten to drive the ambulance while a law enforcement ranger was doing CPR on some guy in the back, and he told me all about it while he drove. He'd been so excited, he'd hit the gas before everyone was fully loaded in the back, and someone had fallen out, but luckily hadn't been hurt. I asked Guy to let me out at my dorm. He seemed confused that I wasn't going directly to the ambulance, but I didn't want to explain that I was delaying the rescue for a sandwich.

I ran up the three flights of stairs, tripping over my boots, justifying the detour by telling myself that boosting my blood sugar would improve my job performance in the long run. I grabbed a bagel and the last hunk of a baby loaf of mild cheddar I found in the communal fridge, along with a handful of Pepto-Bismol chewable tablets. These emergency response jobs always gave me heartburn. I got my climbing harness and helmet, too, because Stefan would be pissed if he ended up having to loan me gear when he was part of the contingent that was always telling me I should be prepared for anything. I skidded back down the stairs, feeling great with my little blue backpack full of food and gear.

The garbageman called again with the same information: car

over the embankment. I jogged back to the ambulance and headed down the hill. There wasn't any traffic. I tuned the radio to the only station we get in Paradise, the Funky Monkey. It's a hard rock station, but for some reason it was playing the Postal Service: "Don't wake me, I plan on sleeping in." I turned it up, dedicating the song to my upset stomach. Comm. Center called again and said that there was a law enforcement ranger, Chris Trotter, who could respond to the accident as well, but she was an hour away.

For a moment I missed having a partner. It wasn't as nice showing up by myself. I didn't think it inspired as much confidence, seeing my lone silhouette on the horizon instead of a rescue posse, squad, team, crew, or whatever. A partner would also make me braver and stronger. Someone who would say, "Don't worry, Bree, I've got your back," as they did a kung-fu move and grinned. I rubbed the ambulance's dashboard and said, "We've been through a lot together, huh?" But somehow it didn't seem like the same sort of thing. In silence, I ate my bagel and the cheese and two bubble packs of Pepto-Bismol tablets, with one hand on the wheel.

I parked the ambulance behind a garbage truck blocking the road. I could see a man lying right on the double yellow stripe in front of the truck. There wasn't any damage to the barrier, so I figured maybe the garbageman had just run over this guy. That would be easy. Maybe he was already dead, and there was nothing for me to do here; I could go back and finish the floors.

He wasn't dead. I saw him move a little through the windshield as I set the emergency brake. My heart sank, not because I wished he were dead, but because I knew the fun daydream where I saved everybody before four-thirty was over, and the work was beginning. I sat for a second, regaining composure and slowing down my heart rate. I resorted to the disposition I've perfected over years of ambulance driving. Sort of a sour, jaded, heartless routine that is amazingly efficient at getting the job done, but sadly, lacks the heady giddiness of an adrenaline rush. I turned on all the flashing emergency lights so that nobody would run into the ambulance if they came around the corner, then grabbed the barely portable orange first-aid kit out of the back and lugged it towards the garbage truck.

The debilitated man was lying about two feet in front of the truck. I kept walking till I was standing over him. I didn't want to kneel at his level just yet, to get too close and involved without knowing what the problem was. I looked down at him with my hands in my pockets and the ambulance's jump kit on my back. He was young, and he looked Hispanic. Maybe in his early twenties. His clothes were dirty and wet, but I didn't see any blood anywhere.

"Did you get run over by this garbage truck?" I asked bluntly, almost accusingly.

"No," he replied calmly and with an air of resignation.

"Then why are you lying in the middle of the road?" I was going for a scolding tone, but it came out flat, like a good traffic cop. "You've clearly upset the driver, and you're blocking traffic." I gestured towards an imaginary backup behind the ambulance. The road probably wouldn't see another car for over an hour.

"Well," the man said, without attempting to move out of the way, "yesterday afternoon my girlfriend and I were taking pictures of each other out on the point, down that little trail by the edge of the cliff, just over the fence. I couldn't get enough of the scenery in the picture so I asked her to take one more step backwards, and she did, but she fell over the edge." He drew a ragged breath and then continued as I listened, expressionless, my hands still in my pockets.

"I freaked out," he said. "I yelled for her, but she didn't answer. I ran back to the road, but nobody was coming and my cell phone didn't work, so I decided to climb down to her. I got most of the way down the side of the cliff next to the waterfall, but it kept getting steeper, and it was mossy and wet, and then I slipped and fell off the cliff down into the water at the bottom right next to her. I broke both my legs and my left wrist." He showed me his wrist, cradled against his chest. I nodded and smiled politely, encouraging him to continue.

"My girlfriend was pretty fucked up when I crawled over to her. She landed on the rocks, not in the water, but she was conscious and everything. I tried yelling for a while, but we couldn't hear if any cars came by, and I think the waterfall noise drowned us out, anyways. It got dark, and she couldn't move at all because of the pain, so I curled up next to her and our clothes froze on us during the night and, y'know, it sucked." He looked at me and I had perfect empathy for the freezing, fucked-up night thing, but he wouldn't have known it.

"This morning," he went on, "I knew she was going to die, and it was freakin' cold and nobody was going to come looking for us, so I decided I had to crawl out. I floated down the stream below the falls for a while and then used my good arm and inched up the slope on the downhill side. I started just before dawn, and I knew it had taken me hours to get to this road. Nobody was coming, and I didn't want anyone to drive by me, so I crawled out into the middle of the road, and a minute later this garbage truck came barreling around the blind corner and almost hit me."

I turned around and looked at the truck, and then at the deaf garbage truck driver. He waved at me from the truck cab where he was still manning the radio, and I waved back. "All that, and to be killed by a garbage truck." He said, rolling his eyes, "That was a close one."

"So," I asked, "your girlfriend is still at the bottom of the waterfall?"

"Yes," he said, looking focused again.

"OK," I nodded. "I'm just going to call this in on the radio."

It took me a few seconds to figure out how to condense the story, but I decided on: "Comm. Center, 686. I'm at Christine Falls. No car went over the embankment, but there are two patients who fell over the falls, one with leg fractures who is now back on the road and one with unknown injuries who is at the bottom of Christine Falls. Ask Stefan to come down here with the rigging equipment, and anybody else who might be around and willing to help."

I nodded and smiled at the man in front of the garbage truck. "They'll send some folks real soon." I said. He didn't look reassured: even with my tough-guy routine I'm still just a sunburnt girl with a ponytail.

I said, "I'm going to take a quick look at your legs, then." I looked down at them. "Yeah, they look broken. Can you wiggle your toes?"

I took off his shoes, and his feet were black with frostbite. The garbage man scavenged him a blanket from the cab of his truck. Then we all sat around because I didn't want to leave the man in the road until somebody else showed up who could care for him. I felt calm, standing in the sunshine, happy, almost, for the lull, but my stomach was still killing me.

Chris Trotter showed up sooner than I'd thought she would. She'd turned on the emergency lights on her law enforcement SUV to make all the RVs and deer get out of her way. She had come as fast as she could, and she was revved and happy to be there. I, on the other hand, had reached the point where I was nauseated thinking about what was coming next. I liked being needed, in a desperate, time-critical, life or death, adrenaline-pumping sort of way. It was flattering. But another part of my brain stood back and wondered how much chaos one person could take. Maybe I felt this way because in this job I was only needed when something had already gone wrong, and there was nobody else to send. This kind

of situation inspired dread, or heartburn. In terms of rescue spe-
cialists, when the park sent somebody else they knew they had me
as a second-string backup, but when they sent me it was because
there was no one else.

I told Chris what had happened and that we needed to get
two ambulances started from Tacoma, which at about an hour and
a half away was the nearest city. We were also going to need about
six people who knew how to rig up a way of getting the girlfriend
back up the cliff, as well as another first-aid kit, because the one I
had with me sucked. I told her the boyfriend needed to be back-
boarded and he needed his own EMT, because I needed to go see
about the girlfriend.

Chris said she was going to take command of the situation,
unless I wanted it. I didn't think she was serious. I think the Park
Service has some kind of certification you have to get before you
can be in charge. There's probably a form I'd have to fill out, which
would have to be signed by my supervisor.

I went back to the ambulance and got my harness and helmet
out from between the two front seats. I was digging around in the
pockets of my pack to see if I had any more Pepto-Bismol stashed
when Stefan drove up in his dusty blue Volvo, crammed full of gear
from the SAR cache in Paradise. I grabbed a rope from him, and he
went to get the story from Chris so they could discuss big-picture
management things.

I shuffled down the trail towards the edge of the cliff, carrying
the ridiculously large first-aid kit, the rope, and my personal gear. A
couple of middle-aged male tourists were leaning against the hood
of their black Cadillac Escalade next to Stefan's car, checking out the
flashing lights and the garbage truck and taking in the whole picture.
They asked me if I wanted any help. I smiled and yelled, "Sure, come
over here and take this first-aid kit, it's really heavy."

The two men followed me down the well-used trail to where

the earth dropped off. The edge was sloping and mossy, and on one side there was a dirty gully that looked like it channeled a lot of runoff after rains. I couldn't see anybody down over the edge. All I could see was a bend in the stream below the falls, and some bushes on the opposite bank. I yelled a few times, but I couldn't hear anybody.

I put my harness on while the two men watched me, and then I wrapped one end of the rope around a slender, smooth-skinned tree that was relatively close to the edge. I wrapped it around four times, because I was going for friction, and then I tied a bowline back around the rope. It doesn't take any hardware to secure the rope this way, which was good because I didn't have any.

I clipped the abhorrently large first-aid kit to the back of my harness with a plastic ice-screw organizer I'd been too lazy to take off earlier in the year. The weight was awkward and pulled me backwards. I started to rappel down over the edge, but one of the two tourists started yelling at me and messing with my knot, so I stopped. He said the knot had started to pull, but I looked at it and saw that it was just tightening up against the tree's smooth bark. I told him that the knot was good, but that I needed him to stay there and make sure that nobody messed with it, because this was a life or death matter. I gave him a look like I trusted him with everything so he'd better not screw up. I could see his posture improve. He felt important. My knot was safe. I left.

It was really loose in the gully and a lot of dirt fell down in my shirt and my boots. Maneuvering with the first-aid kit was difficult.

When I got to the bottom there was no body there. I walked out into the stream. The water was freezing as it poured in around my ankles. I shivered, and shook the dirt out of my jacket before zipping it up. I started walking upstream toward the falls, and then I saw her on a small sandbar next to the base of the waterfall, lying on her back, awkwardly, between several large round rocks.

She was facing away from me with one arm up in the air, holding her cell phone over her head. There isn't any cell phone service in the park except on top of the mountain, so I figured she probably wasn't having any luck. When I was right next to her I yelled, "Hi!" over the roar of the water. She screamed and dropped her phone.

"Sorry," she said, "you startled me."

"What are you doing?" I asked her.

"I'm trying to figure out how to save a text message of my last words."

"OK," I replied. "I'm just going to call in on the radio to say that I found you, and then we'll see what we can do about getting you back out of here." There wasn't any sun down in the deep gorge below the falls, and my fingers were cold. It was hard to feel the radio in my hand. Andy had been here at this exact spot two weeks earlier because another woman had fallen over these falls, and I wished I'd asked him more about the extraction details. I couldn't hear the radio, so I just pushed the transmit button and said I'd found the woman, that she was alive, and that I needed another EMT as soon as one could be rustled up. And that the woman would need to be raised out in a litter.

"OK," I said again, patting her arm, "they're going to have all the details figured out in a minute. How are you doing?"

She was shivering, and I looked for some chemical hot packs in the kit, but there weren't any. The kit was shitty. When I'd opened it in the parking lot, the zipper had broken off in my hand. I couldn't find anything I needed in it, and it looked like it hadn't been used in years. It probably hadn't. I was pissed I hadn't brought the one from the CIC that I'd put together a few weeks before. I gave her my green polarfleece jacket, tucking it around her shoulders.

There was a lot of blood on the rocks around her, but I couldn't find where the blood had come from. I could see the bone in her elbow sticking out of the skin, but it didn't look like it had bled much. Not even the edges of her torn sweatshirt were saturated. She had on tight hip-hugger jeans and a belt with multicolored rhinestones. "Nice belt," I said.

"Old Navy. Eight dollars," she told me.

Her thigh had a U-bend in the middle of the femur, and her leg was sticking out in a weird direction. Despite this, she looked OK for the most part. I think if a person survives all night in freezing temperatures while wearing wet cotton after a sixty-foot fall and landing on rocks at the base of a waterfall, they are probably going to live.

I told her as much, and said I'd take her phone for safekeeping just in case. She wanted to know if her boyfriend had made it back out. I said it sounded like he'd floated downstream for a while and then he'd crawled up the embankment and out to the road, where he'd flagged down a garbage truck. Now, I said, he was probably sitting in the back of the ambulance with the heat cranked up, and loads of pain medication.

She said she loved him for saving her, but hated him for being warm right now when she wasn't.

"Yeah, well," I said, "true love is always kind of a love-hate thing anyway. That's how it goes sometimes. Being cold just makes you appreciate being warm that much more. Just think about how much you'll appreciate the little things after this, like hot showers and hot chocolate and hot water bottles and—"

"Do you mind?!" She yelled over the noise of the waterfall. She was smiling, though.

"And hot tubs, heaters, electric blankets, hot men." I shut up for a minute. I looked up to see if anybody else was coming down, but there was no sign of anyone at the top of the cliff at all.

I wondered what was going on up there. It takes a couple of people who do this sort of thing often to remember how to set up the ropes and the pulley systems. I remembered Andy telling me that during the rescue here two weeks ago he hadn't been able to find enough people who knew what they were doing. Chris had been in charge, just like today, and she'd asked a couple of volunteers to help out. They'd said they knew what to do, but then they'd done it all wrong, and Andy, worried he was about to die, had scrambled up the side of the cliff, redone everything practically by himself, and then rappelled back down so that he could get hauled back up, carrying the patient in the litter. At least I knew Stefan was up there, somewhere, setting things up. He could do it all by himself if he had to. Then he could teach the garbage truck driver and the people in the Escalade how to operate the system.

I looked behind me, back towards the gully I'd rappelled down. There was Stefan, hauling some gear around the corner. "Stefan! Who's setting up the rigging system?"

"Aw," he yelled back, "they've got it covered."

"Great," I yelled, "why don't you go up with the patient then?" He said he'd do it, and I was relieved.

"Were you just in the park for the day, or was this part of a longer trip?" I asked the woman at the bottom of the waterfall.

"Just for the day, on leave. We're both Army medics. Going to ship out to Iraq in two months." I tried not to look skeptical, what with the leg situation, and I asked her if she wanted to go. She looked too young. Less than eighteen, blond, and wearing too much make-up, which had run all over her face. She looked like she belonged in a mall. I was amazed she'd chosen to come to a national park on her leave at all. Maybe it had been her boyfriend's choice.

"Oh yeah, I'm excited. Going to see the world, pay for college, do something interesting."

"Well," I said, "that sounds like it'll be just great. Hey," I added, "we're going to have to straighten out your leg so we can get you into the litter and back up the cliff." She looked shocked. "Look, if we don't then it'll hang out and bounce around, get caught on bushes, and I'm sure you don't want that, either." While I talked, I cut up her pantleg to the waist. I could see that her hip was blue, and the top of her hipbone was sticking out of the skin. I wondered if she'd broken her pelvis.

Andy had said he'd used a full-body vacuum splint on the woman here two weeks ago. I'd never seen a full-body splint, but if we had one, then I wanted it. "Hey, Stefan! Can you ask Chris to send down the full-body vacuum splint?"

"A what?" he yelled back.

"Full-body vacuum splint, we've got one, I swear."

The splint showed up a few minutes later in the arms of Ed Dunlevey, the head of EMS in the park. Ed was beaming. He looked thrilled to have an opportunity to get out of his park police car for a few hours. He was still wearing his bulletproof vest under his shirt, and his gun belt with a myriad of gun accoutrements all smashed up under a very tight-looking, brand-new climbing harness. He had a white plastic helmet on that had never been used before, and his gray wispy hair was sticking out of the ventilation holes.

The full-body vacuum splint itself was large and red; it looked like an oversized dog bed. It came with a yellow plastic hand pump to suck the air out of it. Stefan looked at it and shrugged. In one of the splint's corners were written directions, and so I sat down with it across my lap to read them. It looked simple enough. Now that there were three of us, we could all pick her up together. We'd drape the splint over the litter, then put her in it, and then suck all the air out of the splint, and it would magically conform to her like a full-body cast.

Meanwhile, the paramedics from Tacoma had showed up, and I asked Stefan if one of them could be sent down to give her something for the pain. Stefan went back around the corner to talk on the radio. When he came back, he said that only one of the paramedics could give pain medications, but that guy was afraid of heights, so the other guy was coming down.

"Why is he coming down if he can't help?" I asked.

Stefan shrugged again. Everybody wants to feel important, and I guess sometimes it's more work trying to talk people out of helping than it is to go with the flow and deal with the consequences later. Sometimes, however, it's not.

The medic was huge, probably over three hundred pounds. He was lowered down the cliff to us with his white uniform already drenched in sweat under his arms and covered in dirt down the front. He looked like he was clutching the rope in front of him with all his might. He didn't put his legs toward the cliff to walk himself down; he just slid down with his face to the dirt. When he reached the bottom, he fell in the water and I had to help him up and hold his elbow while we walked over to the accident site.

When we got there he said he couldn't help because he couldn't give pain medication. "OK," I said. "It was brave of you to come down here, though. Can you help us lift her onto the litter, maybe support her leg? I know if I do it I'll probably bump it or something." He looked pleased to have a job. His whole body was shaking in ripples with excitement. I thought it was an odd effect, and I couldn't help staring at him.

"OK," I said, looking pointedly at Stefan, but talking to the woman, "now we're going to pick you up and move you over into the litter, and it's going to hurt a lot." I narrowed my eyes at Stefan and Ed. "But we're not going to stop no matter what, because we've got to move you over and it'll suck worse if we have to do it twice." Silently to myself, I added, "Because then you'll know what's coming."

She screamed a lot when we picked her up and moved her. It was ungainly and ugly, like it always is. It's disconcerting to me that when I'm right next to someone who is screaming in unmitigated and prolonged agony, it doesn't hurt me a bit. Being that close to suffering, I think my brain does a kind of reboot, bypassing my conscious self, sort of like, "What was that? Wow. She must be in a nasty spot. Wait . . . I'm here too. Am I OK?" It grates on the nerves. I have to remind myself that I am the calm in the face of the storm. I am the rock. I am the one who did not fall over the waterfall in a "Hey babe, take one more step back so you'll fit in the picture." "Ack. I'm falling!" Splat. "Oh shit!" accident.

Finally, somebody on top of the cliff threw down ropes and lowered the litter, an ancient metal contraption in the shape of a lidless wire sarcophagus. We have a nicer one, an orange fiberglass litter that comes apart in two pieces so it's easy to carry, but this wasn't it. True to his word, Stefan tied himself into the rope next to the litter so that he could be pulled up with it and keep the whole thing from scraping and bouncing up the side of the cliff. "Bye," I told the girl. "I'm putting your phone here in your pocket."

Once they were headed up, I needed to figure out how to get Ed and the medic back up to the top of the cliff. The beginning of the gully was a bit steep to climb out, even with a belay, but there weren't any people left at the top of the cliff to pull us up, so I didn't have a lot of options.

I said, "Ed, could you put your rappel device back on the rope and then sort of pull yourself up, and then lock yourself off with your other hand so you don't slide back down, and get up that way?"

"Sure," said Ed, beaming. "I can do it!"

"OK," I said, "when you get to the top I'll tie the medic into the end of the rope and then you can belay him up while he tries to climb out on his own. That way he'll have two hands," I added, looking at the medic. He nodded appreciatively.

As Ed started up, I noticed that the medic's harness didn't fit him at all. His gut spilled out over the buckle and at his hip level, the narrowest part of him where the harness actually connected, the end of the belt was barely threaded through the buckle, never mind doubled back with two inches of tail like the directions tell you. I was surprised it hadn't come apart on him on the way down. I flashed on an extremely disturbing image of this medic, suddenly freed from all constraints except gravity, plunging backwards towards me, myself looking up and seeing him fall, with his huge white medic shirt with the little gold badges flapping in the wind and blocking out the sun. It would never happen that way, I thought to myself reasonably. There wasn't any sun down here for him to block.

"Hey," I said to the medic, "you don't fit in that harness. We're going to have to find some way of making it bigger or making it tighter, or else you might fall out of it on the way up. I'm amazed you didn't fall out on the way down here." The medic was already highly agitated. Sweat was dripping off the end of his nose, and he was breathing in short, hard gasps. There was no way of telling if the news that he'd narrowly escaped plummeting to his demise affected him at all. Maybe he wouldn't have died, I thought, still staring at his waistline. After all, the woman we'd just sent off in the litter hadn't. Neither had her boyfriend, or the woman who fell over this waterfall two weeks ago.

"Suck it in," I said, and grabbed the end of the harness belt, pulling as hard as I could. He came with me, and I had to push my elbow into his gut to maintain some counter-pressure. My elbow went way in. I was surprised.

"Hey," said the medic, looking down at me, "if we both get out of this alive, would you have dinner with me?"

"No," I said. "Here, suck it in as hard as you can." I wrenched on the end of the harness, and managed to get another inch or two out of it. Now it doubled back, and there was a bit of tail sticking out the other side of the buckle. Good enough for government work.

Ed had made it to the top. "Hey, Ed, you ready to belay up

the medic?" Ed gave me an enthusiastic wave and a thumbs-up. The medic started up then, sending a shower of dirt and rocks down on me. To get out of the fall line I walked back around the corner to grab all the stuff that had been left behind. There was a lot. I packed up the first-aid kit, the yellow vacuum pump, and the excess patient-packaging materials, the webbing and all the other crap that had showed up after it was no longer needed. I tied it all to my harness with a piece of webbing. When I came back around the corner I was relieved that there was no sign of Ed or the medic, which I assumed meant that everything had gone OK. I hand-over-handed it back up the rope. The weight of all the equipment hanging and swinging between my legs made it difficult going, and by the time I'd made it to the top everybody else was gone.

I picked up my green Park Service fleece jacket that someone had left next to a pile of ropes at the top of the cliff, and put it back on. There was no one around, so I went back up the little trail to the parking lot and found Chris doing paperwork in her patrol car. "Hey, Chris," I said, "you need me to help with anything else?"

"No, they're going to fly her out, the helicopter will be here in a minute. We're just trying to get the people who are parked here out of the way right now. Stefan says he'll drop the gear off later, so you can put it away." I put the first-aid kit back in the ambulance and headed up the hill, out of the way, back to another task, to the next thing on the list. On the way back to Paradise, the Funky Monkey contributed Dave Matthews's "Eat, drink, and be merry, for tomorrow we die."

The woman had left a little blood on my jacket. Back at the dorm, I pulled the screwdriver out of it, tossed the jacket in my laundry pile, and stuck the screwdriver in my pants pocket. I had guessed right this morning—it was warm enough without a jacket, now that the sun was high overhead. I was hungry again. I grabbed a bagel from the communal fridge and found some cream cheese to smear on it, and then walked back up to the climbers' self-registration box eating my bagel in the sun. When I got there I pulled out the screwdriver and started back in on the Plexiglas display cover.

There were a few cars in the lot. A couple of tourists strolled by and took a picture of the mountain with the Paradise Old Station and the self-registration box and me with the screwdriver in the foreground. I'm sure the whole tableau was beautiful, and apparently the tourists thought so, too, because the man asked me if I would take a picture of him and his wife standing right where I had been.

"Sure is quiet here, you must really enjoy your job," said the woman, handing me her camera.

"Yeah, I'm lucky," I said, and I realized that I was. I put my eye up to the viewfinder and said, "Just take one more step backwards so I can get you and the scenery in the picture," but I was the only one who thought it was funny.

AFTERWORD

It's autumn again. A new fall. A few years down the road. In the months after Charlie died, almost all the climbing rangers who had worked with me on the south side of the mountain got married. So did I, wearing a green knee-length skirt and with flowers in my hair. Then I bought a pre-depression era house with a bright kitchen across the street from a strawberry field. I can see the mountains from the main road, but they are a long ways off and there are a large number of fields and foothills, fences, old barns, and belted Galloway cows between us.

A lot of things are much the same as they were that last season on Rainier. I still awake, needed in the middle of the night, but now my ear is attuned to the soft chirps my little daughter makes rooting in her sleep rather than the reverberations of human chaos caused by ice fall, rock fall, trip 'n falls, tempests, and avalanches. I still anxiously await springtime, but now it's because I want to know if my collard greens, arugula, and daffodils will grow, and not because I'm afraid I'll get frostbite or die this year.

Asked by my editor to add an afterword to my book, I can only offer that neither of my twin philosophies, that shared hardship increases camaraderie nor the doctrine "that which doesn't kill you makes you stronger," worked out for me. The mountain irrevocably broke me in many ways, but it also kept me focused on what I wanted in my life: good friends to grow old with. Along with a strong desire to grow old generally. If this experience had been the sum of my life, then this book would have outlined a tragedy. Fortunately, it was only a summer job I had for three years in my early twenties.

And now I have a husband who looks out for me, family and friends who support me. People I found as much through shared joys as shared hardships. Crazily enough, climbing is once again something I do for fun with the people I love.

ABOUT THE AUTHOR

BREE LOEWEN DISCOVERED CLIMBING when she joined a volunteer search and rescue group at age 15. Through a series of adventures and misadventures she has climbed in Alaska, Canada, Mexico, and various South American countries, as well as all over the western U.S.

After years of living out of her car she now resides with her husband Russell and daughter Vivian in Carnation, Washington. On clear days she can see Mount Rainier from her front porch. On cloudy ones she can see its image on the license plate of her car, as the backdrop of evening newscasts, and reflected in the eyes of every hiker in plastic boots climbing Mt. Si in the early days of spring.

She continues to enjoy all types of climbing along with sea kayaking, volunteering for Seattle Mountain Rescue, restoring her 1920's craftsman style bungalow, and baking fruit pies.

OTHER TITLES YOU MIGHT ENJOY BY
THE MOUNTAINEERS BOOKS

FORGET ME NOT
A Memoir
Jennifer Lowe-Anker; foreword by Jon Krakauer
An insightful and at times wrenching memoir of
love lost and love found, set against a backdrop
of the world's tallest peaks

CHASING WAVES
A Surfer's Tale of
Obsessive Wandering
Amy Waeschle
Chasing Waves is a traveler's tale of
searching for adventure and surf along
some of the most remote coastlines and
corners of the world.

HIGH INFATUATION
A Climber's Guide to Love and Gravity
Steph Davis
One of the most accomplished female climbers
in the world affirms the joy of following your
dreams and passions—and explores what it
means to live a truly adventurous life.

SPIRITED WATERS
Soloing South Through
the Inside Passage
Jennifer Hahn
A gripping account of an unforgettable
and challenging solo kayaking journey